SPECTRUM®

Geography

Grade 4

Spectrum®

An imprint of Carson-Dellosa Publishing LLC
Greensboro, North Carolina

Photo credits: Library of Congress, LC-USZ62-131447:
page 36; Library of Congress, LC-USZ62-57309: page 85
U.S. Navy, PH1(AW) William R. Goodwin, page 91

Spectrum®
An imprint of Carson-Dellosa Publishing LLC
P.O. Box 35665
Greensboro, NC 27425 USA

                    ISBN 0-7696-8724-5

06-213127811

Table of Contents

The Great Lakes

LESSON 6

LESSON 7

The Upper Plains

LESSON 8

The Southeast

LESSON 9

LESSON 10

The Southwest

The Rocky Mountains

The Far West

Reading a Globe

Maps and globes are different models of Earth. Both represent the real Earth at a size people can use easily. Figures 1 and 2 show Earth like a globe. A **globe** is a small model of Earth. A globe imitates the round shape of our planet.

A **map** is a flat model of Earth. The map in Figure 3 tries to "open up" the round globe and show it as a flat map. One problem with flat maps is that distances and directions sometimes look different than they really are.

Any one side of a globe shows only part of Earth. With a map, you can see all of Earth at once. Look at the globes in Figures 1 and 2. See if you can find some of the same places on the map in Figure 3.

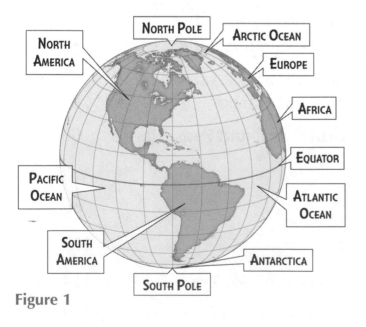

Figure 1

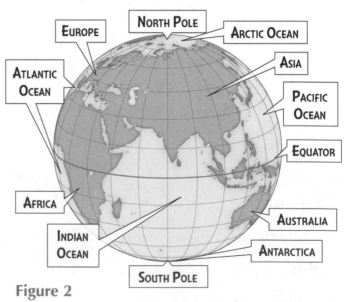

Figure 2

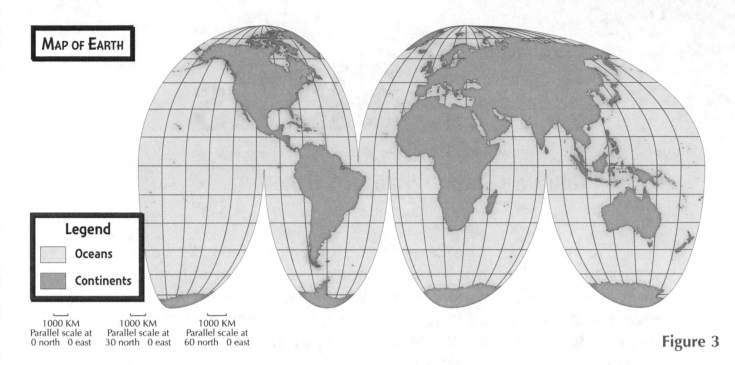

MAP OF EARTH

Legend
Oceans
Continents

1000 KM
Parallel scale at
0 north   0 east

1000 KM
Parallel scale at
30 north   0 east

1000 KM
Parallel scale at
60 north   0 east

Figure 3

Find the equator on the globes. The **equator** is an imaginary line drawn around the center of a globe or map of Earth. The names of the seven **continents** (large land masses) and four **oceans** (large areas of water) are also given on the globes in Figures 1 and 2. Find the **North Pole** and **South Pole** on the globes. These are the most northern and southern points on Earth.

Because maps and globes cannot be the same size as Earth, they are drawn to **scale.** A scale shows how much smaller the map is than the real world. A map's **title** tells you what the map is about. **Symbols** are drawings, lines, or dots that stand for something else. The **legend** explains what each symbol on the map or globe means.

Maps and globes have many uses. They can help us find our way around as we travel. Scientists use maps to predict the weather. Can you think of some other ways that we use maps?

What can a map or a globe tell you about what it is like to live in a certain place? Consider that places near the equator have the hottest weather on Earth. The weather gradually gets cooler as you travel toward the North Pole or South Pole from the equator.

Build Your
Map Skills

Read a Climate Map of Earth

The symbol that looks like a star on Figure 4 is called a compass rose. A **compass rose** is a map symbol that shows directions. This compass rose shows the four main **cardinal directions** (north, south, east, and west). It also shows **intermediate directions,** which are northwest, northeast, southwest, and southeast.

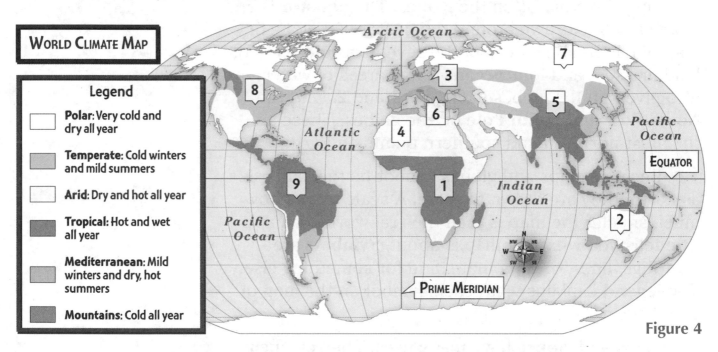

WORLD CLIMATE MAP

Legend

	Polar: Very cold and dry all year
	Temperate: Cold winters and mild summers
	Arid: Dry and hot all year
	Tropical: Hot and wet all year
	Mediterranean: Mild winters and dry, hot summers
	Mountains: Cold all year

Figure 4

The map lines that are drawn parallel to the equator are called lines of **latitude.** The **prime meridian** is an imaginary line drawn from the North Pole to the South Pole. The lines drawn parallel to the prime meridian are called lines of **longitude.** For more information, see Appendix page 100.

This map is a climate map. **Climate** refers to the typical weather of a specific place on Earth. Several factors affect climate:

Latitude: At the equator, the sun's rays hit at a direct angle. This makes the air temperature very hot. As you move toward the poles, the Sun's rays become cooler due to the curved surface of Earth.

Altitude: It is usually cool on top of a mountain even in summer. This is because a mountaintop is at a high **altitude.**

Winds: Winds from hot areas of Earth raise temperatures and those from cold areas lower temperatures. Winds influence the amount of **precipitation** (rain or snow) each area gets.

Distance from the sea: Land near the sea has more moderate seasons than areas that are inland.

The climate map shows six different climate zones. Notice that there are numbers on the map in different climate zones. In the table, write the name of the continent where the number is located. Then, write a description of the climate.

	Continent	Description of the Climate
1	Africa	Tropical (hot and wet all year)
2	Australia	Arid (Dry and hot all year)
3	Europe	Temperate (Cold winters and mild summers)
4	Africa	Arid (Dry and hot all year)
5		
6		
7		
8		
9		

Explore the World's Oceans

Something to Think About

How can you describe a trip over the world's oceans?

As you have learned, the oceans and continents look different depending upon which side of the globe you are viewing. In this activity, each globe shows you a different view of the world. You will label some of the continents and oceans on each globe. Then, you will use the globes to explore the world's oceans.

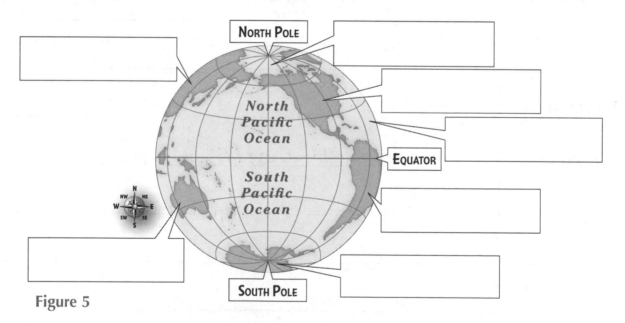

Figure 5

Use Figure 5 to explore the oceans and continents.

1. Fill in the boxes on Figure 5 to label the world's continents and oceans. If you need to, refer to page 2.

2. Plan your trip. Start at the southern tip of South America. From there, draw a line to eastern Australia. The line you draw shows the way you will travel. Answer these questions to describe your trip.

What continent will you pass to the south? _____

What ocean will you cross? _____

What direction will you travel? _____

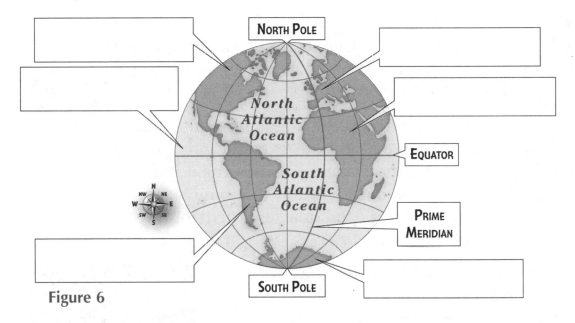

Figure 6

Use Figure 6 to explore the oceans and continents.

3. Fill in the boxes on Figure 6 to label the world's continents and oceans. If you need to, refer to the map on page 2.

4. Plan your trip. Start at the east coast of North America. From there, draw a line to the southern tip of Africa. The line you draw shows the way you will travel. Answer these questions to describe your trip.

What continent will you pass to the west? _____

What ocean will you cross? _____

What direction will you travel? _____

What Are Regions?

Some states within the United States can be grouped together based on things they have in common. States grouped together in this way are called a **region.**

Sometimes, the things the states have in common are based on human activity. For example, the map shows how the U.S. government groups the states together into regions based on the economy. An **economy** is a system of producing and distributing products and services.

Maps are also organized based on the physical characteristics of Earth's surface. States within these physical regions may have a similar climate or similar **landforms,** such as mountains, plains, or deserts.

Organizing the United States into regions allows us to compare different parts of the country and gives us a more complete understanding of the nation as a whole. For example, people in the Middle Atlantic region tend to live or work in large cities. The economy of this area is influenced by important seaports on the Atlantic Ocean.

New York City is a large city in the Middle Atlantic Region.

The Great Lakes region is America's industrial heartland. The area is home to many of the country's largest cities. This region also boasts an important outdoor recreation and tourism industry.

The fertile soil of the flat Plains region produces abundant harvests of grains such as wheat and oats.

The Far West is an area of contrasts. Consider how different the frigid lands of Alaska are from the tropical islands of Hawaii. The long growing seasons have made southern California an important agricultural region. Yet high-tech computer industries are also key parts of the area's economy.

Refer to Appendix pages 98–99 for descriptions of the other regions of the United States shown on the map.

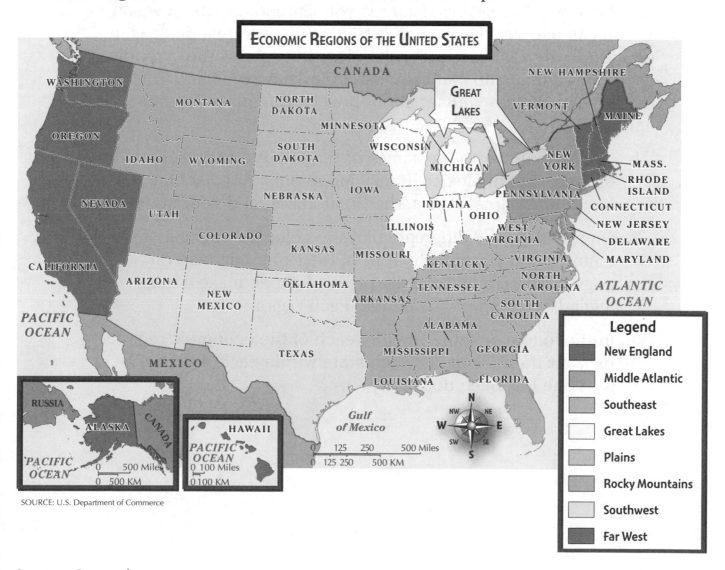

ECONOMIC REGIONS OF THE UNITED STATES

SOURCE: U.S. Department of Commerce

Legend
- New England
- Middle Atlantic
- Southeast
- Great Lakes
- Plains
- Rocky Mountains
- Southwest
- Far West

Build Your

Map Skills

Draw Regions on a Physical Map

This is a physical map of the United States. A **physical map** shows a region's landforms (like mountains and deserts) and water forms (like rivers and lakes). This map also shows state borders, which are human **political boundaries.** These human boundaries are imaginary lines.

This map has several features you learned about in Lesson 1. You can use the compass rose to describe where a place is in relation to another place. The map legend explains the symbols used on the map and can help you understand the map. The map scale will help you see about how far one place is from another.

1. On the map, write the names of the Atlantic and Pacific oceans, Gulf of Mexico, Rocky Mountains, Appalachian Mountains, Great Plains, the Great Lakes, and your state.

2. On the map, use different colors to color the regions of the country you learned about from the economic map on page 9. Then, on a separate piece of paper, make a map legend, with colors, to identify each region.

3. In the following table, identify each of the economic regions on your map. Then, list each state within each region. The first one has been done for you.

Economic Region	States Within Each Region
Far West	Washington, Oregon, Nevada, California, Alaska, Hawaii

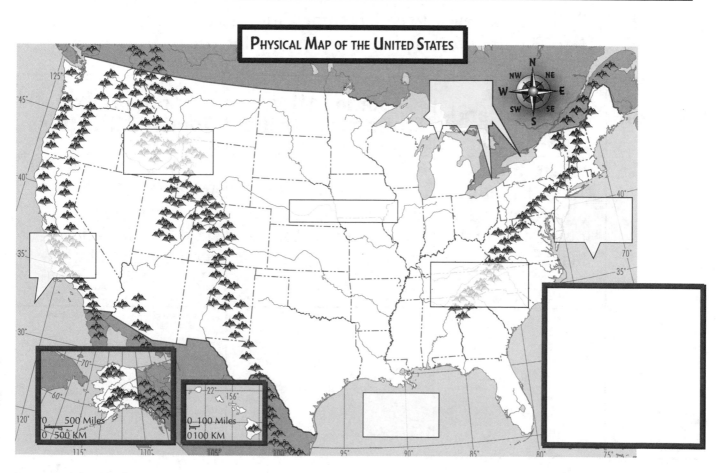

PHYSICAL MAP OF THE UNITED STATES

LESSON 2

Travel to Different Regions of the United States

What makes each region of our country unique?

In this activity, you will collect information about each region of the United States to write a travel book. So, of course, you will need to become an expert on each region of the country! Read pages 8–11 again and do some research using the library. Refer to the climate map on page 4. You will also find some helpful information on Appendix pages 98–99.

1. Use the tables below to collect information about each region. The first item has been completed for you.

Region	Climate (Summer and Winter)	Some Major Economic Activities	Some Major Tourist Attractions
Far West	Climate varies widely. Examples: California: arid; Hawaii: tropical; Alaska: polar	motion picture industry; computer industry; agriculture (fruit and vegetables)	California: Hollywood and Disneyland. Alaska: wonderful scenery. Hawaii: scenery and climate.
Great Lakes			

Region	Climate (Summer and Winter)	Some Major Economic Activities	Some Major Tourist Attractions
Middle Atlantic			
New England			
Southeast			

2. After you have collected all your information, select two regions from the table and write their names below. On a separate piece of paper, write a paragraph for your book describing how the two regions are different.

_____

_____

3. Now, select one of the regions and create a travel poster that reflects that region's characteristics. You will use the poster to help sell your book in bookstores located throughout that region. On a separate piece of paper, organize the pictures and text that will go on your poster.

The New England Region

The New England region of the United States includes six states: Maine, New Hampshire, Vermont, Massachusetts, Rhode Island, and Connecticut. It is the smallest region of the United States, but it has had a huge impact on our country. Many of the first European settlers in America landed in New England. They helped establish the region's political format—the town meeting. At town meetings, New Englanders gather to discuss and vote on important issues. The region is also a world leader in higher education.

The Atlantic Ocean has been an important part of the region's economy since colonial times. Early merchants used the ocean to transport goods to and from Europe. Trade and commerce drove the region's economy until the mid-1800s. Then, manufacturing became important, particularly in Connecticut, Rhode Island, and Massachusetts. By the 1950s, the region's economy began to shift to service businesses. (**Service businesses** do work that directly benefits others.) These include financial, insurance, and retail companies.

The financial district in Boston, Massachusetts.

Three of the four most densely populated states in the United States are in New England: Rhode Island, Massachusetts, and Connecticut. Since colonial times, many immigrants to America first entered the country here. Many decided to stay, giving southern New England a wide **diversity,** or a variety of people from different backgrounds.

Northern New England is mainly rural. This area includes much of Maine, New Hampshire, and Vermont. Canada forms the northern border. New York State lies to the west, and the Atlantic Ocean forms the eastern boundary. This rugged region has cold lakes and streams, rocky coastlines, and a huge expanse of forest. The rural economy depends on dairy and poultry farms, maple syrup production, fishing, and tourism. The timber industry is also an important part of Maine's economy.

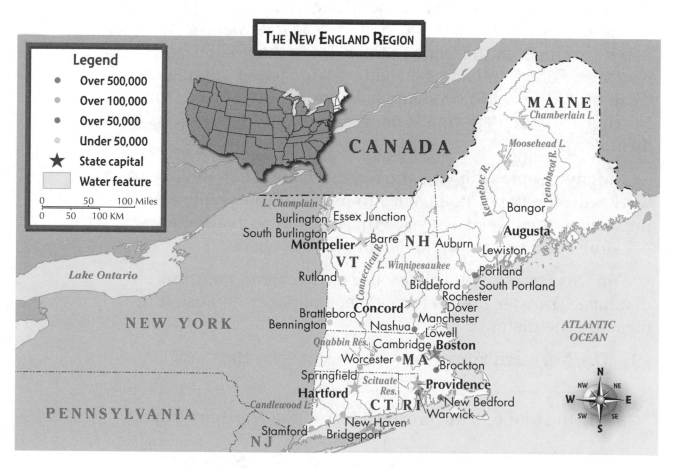

THE NEW ENGLAND REGION

Legend
- Over 500,000
- Over 100,000
- Over 50,000
- Under 50,000
★ State capital
Water feature

0   50   100 Miles
0   50   100 KM

Build Your
Map Skills

Use a Special-Purpose Map

The Northern Forest is the largest area of unbroken forest in the eastern United States. It covers more than 25 million acres in northern New England and southeastern Canada. Many lakes, rivers, and mountains lie in the forest, and its rugged terrain has discouraged widespread settlement. Still, nearly 1 million people live and work in rural communities in and near the forest.

The region's economy has long been dominated by the paper and timber industry. At one time, Maine was the leading paper producer in the United States. More than half of the Northern Forest, in fact, is owned by large paper companies. Changes in the world economy have brought change to the Northern Forest. Paper mills have closed and forestry jobs have dwindled.

Many people who love the Northern Forest would like to work with the paper companies to preserve jobs while also preserving the forest. They see tourism and recreation as a possible source of jobs and income for the region.

In this lesson, you will use the map scale to measure distance. Transfer the scale to a piece of paper and use it to measure the distance.

1. The Northern Forest is in which states on the map?

   _____

2. Which state has the greatest part of the Northern Forest?

   _____

3. Use the map scale to measure the length of the Northern Forest from Lake Ontario to the northeast tip of Maine. About how long is it? About how wide is it at its widest point in the state of Maine?

_____

_____

4. Name one lake and one river that are located within the Northern Forest. In which states are these lakes?

_____

_____

5. Which state capital is located within the Northern Forest?

_____

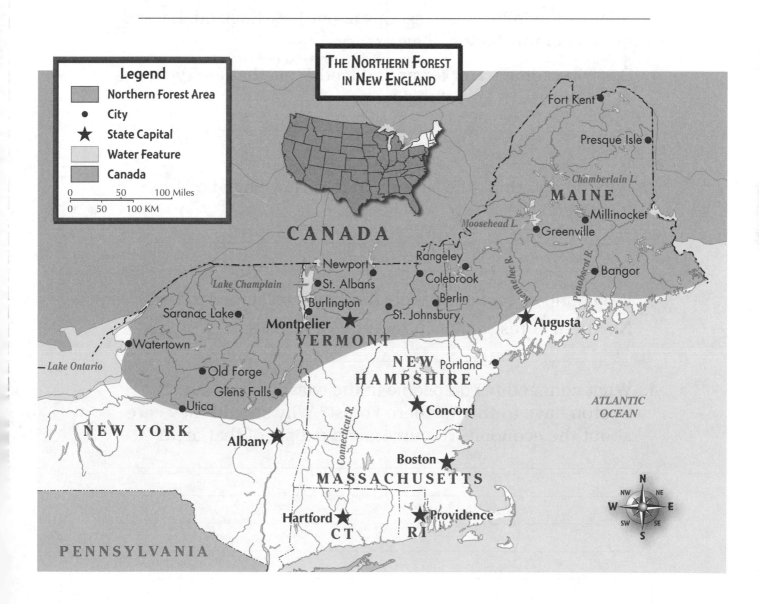

THE NORTHERN FOREST IN NEW ENGLAND

Legend
Northern Forest Area
• City
★ State Capital
Water Feature
Canada

0   50   100 Miles
0   50   100 KM

Learn about New England

Something to Think About

What natural areas near your home are important to you?

Answer the following questions about New England. Reread the material in this lesson, if necessary.

1. Describe some water forms and landforms that are typical of the Northern Forest region.

   _____

2. Why do you think the largest cities in New England are located on the coast?

   _____

   _____

3. What kind of economic problems have developed in the Northern Forest region in recent years? _____

   _____

4. What connections do people in the coastal cities like Boston have to the Northern Forest? Why should they care about the economy, resources, and people of that area?

   _____

   _____

   _____

   _____

   _____

5. Select three New England communities. Each community should be from a different state. Do library research to complete the following table.

Name and State of Community	Population	Main Economic Activities	Nearby Attractions
Montpelier, Vermont	8,035	Vermont state government services; finance, insurance, and real estate	Vermont Statehouse; Vermont Historical Society Museum; Vermont Mountaineers baseball

6. Identify a natural area in your region of the country. Describe it in the space below. As you write, think about these questions: What are the area's attractions? Is it used for recreation or industry? Has there been any change in the way people use the area? Who benefits most from it?

_____

_____

_____

_____

_____

_____

What Is a Watershed?

A **watershed** collects all the water in a drainage area and channels it into the same place. When people use the word *watershed,* they are usually talking about a river and the area that drains into it through creeks and streams. Individual watersheds are usually separated by high landforms like hills or mountains.

All land areas on Earth are part of a watershed. Watersheds are very important to our environment. They provide places for animals to live. Trees, grasses, and other plant life must be preserved to prevent land erosion in a watershed. **Erosion** is the wearing away of the soil.

Pollution comes from many sources. For example, fertilizer is carried into streams by rain from lawns and planted fields. Even untreated wastewater from homes makes its way from the land into small streams and rivers. Pollution within a watershed can spoil drinking water and kill fish and other animals downstream.

The Connecticut River is part of a huge watershed.

The Connecticut River is the longest river in New England. It lies between the Green Mountains of Vermont and the White Mountains of New Hampshire. The Connecticut River drains parts of Connecticut, Massachusetts, New Hampshire, and Vermont. Plant and animal life is abundant, and the region also has some of the best farmland in New England.

There are many dams on the Connecticut River. The first dams were used to float logs downstream. Later, dams were built to supply energy for factories. Most dams no longer supply energy. Today, dams have created problems because they raise the water temperature, hurting certain fish. They also lower the water quality. Dams prevent the spawning runs of fish up the river and reduce the ability of people to use the river for recreation.

There are lots of good reasons to clean up and restore the Connecticut River watershed. Preserving wetlands along the river can help prevent floods. Wetlands also work as natural water purifiers. Increased recreational use from cleaning up the water can increase the value of property in the watershed and help the economy.

What are people doing to restore and preserve the Connecticut River? They are removing many of the unnecessary dams. Dam removal is the only way to completely restore habitat. It opens miles of river for the spawning runs of the salmon. When dams can't be removed, fish ladders can be built around the dams to allow the salmon to travel around them.

Salmon travel upstream to spawn.

Build Your

Map Skills

Read a Watershed Map

The map shows the Connecticut River watershed with tributaries and dams. A **tributary** is a smaller stream that flows into a larger river.

Use the map to answer the following questions.

1. What tributaries enter the river at Wilder Dam?

_____

2. Which dams are shown on tributaries?

_____

_____

_____

3. In which general direction does the Connecticut River flow?

_____

4. Based on the map scale, about how long is the Connecticut River? Into what body of water does the Connecticut River flow?

_____

_____

_____

_____

5. The Connecticut River forms the border between what two states?

_____

6. Name all of the dams shown on the map in the state of Massachusetts.

_____

_____

7. What tributaries enter the Connecticut River within the state of Connecticut?

_____

_____

THE CONNECTICUT RIVER WATERSHED

CANADA

VERMONT

MAINE

NEW HAMPSHIRE

NEW YORK

MASSACHUSETTS

CONNECTICUT

RHODE ISLAND

Nulhegan R.

Upper Ammonoosuc R.

Passumpsic R.

Ammonoosuc R.

White R.

Mascoma R.

Ottauquechee R.

Sugar R.

West R.

Ashuelot R.

Deerfield R.

Millers R.

Westfield R.

Chicopee R.

Farmington R.

Salmon R.

Eightmile R.

Long Island Sound

Connecticut R.

Legend

1 Leesville Dam (Salmon R.)
2 Rainbow Dam (Farmington R.)
3 DSI Dam (Westfield R.)
4 Holyoke Dam
5 Turners Falls Dam
6 Vernon Dam
7 Townshend Dam (West R.)
8 Bellows Falls Dam
9 Wilder Dam
10 Ryegate (Dodge Falls) Dam
11 Comerford Station Dam
12 Moore Reservoir Dam
13 Gilman Project Dam
14 Lower (Canaan) Dam
15 Murphy Dam
16 Moose Falls Dam
— Dam
→ Direction of river flow

0   25   50 Miles
0   25   50 KM

SOURCE: Based on information from the U.S. Fish and Wildlife Service

Restore the River

What problems may be hurting the watershed where you live?

In this activity, you will be working with a conservation group to develop a plan to preserve and restore the Connecticut River. You will collect information to explain to the governments of Vermont, New Hampshire, Connecticut, and Massachusetts why conservation is important. You will write a letter to persuade the government of these states to help pay for your group's plan.

Gather information about the river from pages 20–23. You can also do extra research in the library. Answer the following questions.

1. What things are special about the Connecticut River watershed?

_____

_____

_____

_____

2. Why should people of New England spend money to take care of the Connecticut River watershed?

_____

_____

_____

_____

3. How is the Connecticut River watershed endangered by pollution?

_____

_____

_____

_____

4. What role do dams play on the river? How do they affect the fish?

_____

_____

_____

_____

5. How can people benefit from projects that help the Connecticut River?

_____

_____

_____

_____

_____

6. All the dams on the river probably cannot be torn down. What else can be done to help the salmon travel up the river to spawn?

_____

_____

7. Now, write your letter to the governors on a separate piece of paper. Be sure to use the facts you have gathered to convince the governors that it is important to restore and preserve the Connecticut River.

The Middle Atlantic Region

The states of New York, Pennsylvania, Delaware, Maryland, and New Jersey make up the Middle Atlantic region. Washington, D.C., is also included in this area.

The Atlantic Coastal Plain on the region's eastern edge contains many shallow bays and large natural harbors. Lakes Erie and Ontario (and parts of Canada) border the region to the north. Large forests and coal, oil, and natural gas are found on the Allegheny Plateau in Pennsylvania and in upstate New York.

During colonial times, the region was a center of commerce and agriculture and helped to link the northern and southern colonies. By the early 1800s, New York and Pennsylvania became centers of industry. The spread of industry allowed cities located on rivers and waterways to grow dramatically. New York City on the Hudson River, Baltimore on Chesapeake Bay, and Philadelphia on the Delaware River all became major transportation centers.

Over the past 50 to 60 years, much of the region's heavy industry has moved away. But other businesses, such as publishing, communications, and finance, have become important. The region's farms produce poultry, cattle, dairy products, vegetables, and seafood. New York ranks within the top five states for many agricultural products, such as dairy, apples, cherries, and potatoes.

The Declaration of Independence and U.S. Constitution were signed at Independence Hall in Philadelphia, Pennsylvania.

Most of the Middle Atlantic region is dominated by large urban areas that stretch along the coast from Boston, Massachusetts, to Washington, D.C. About 16 percent of the United States population lives in this area. It is among the most ethnically diverse regions of the United States.

Much of the Revolutionary War was fought in this region. The Declaration of Independence and the Constitution were both written in Philadelphia. Events that happened here long ago unite us today as a people. This is known as our **cultural history.**

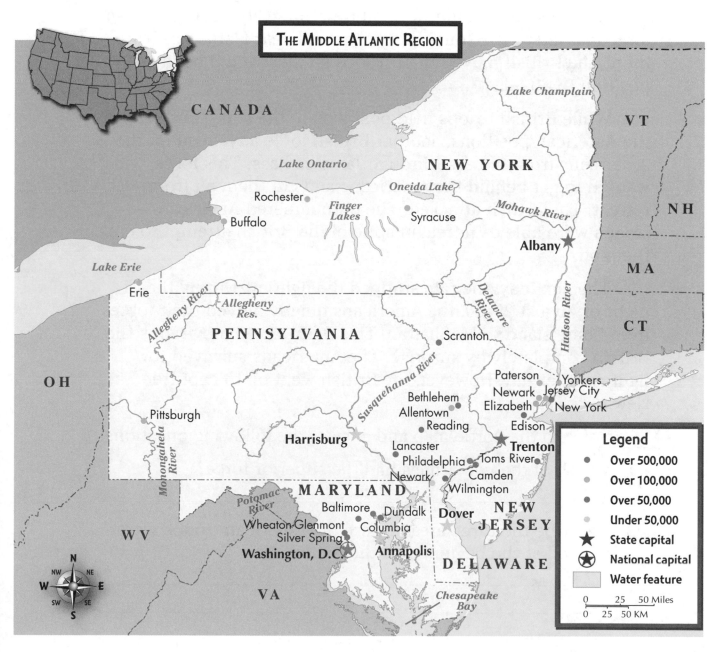

THE MIDDLE ATLANTIC REGION

Legend
- Over 500,000
- Over 100,000
- Over 50,000
- Under 50,000
★ State capital
⊛ National capital
▢ Water feature

0   25   50 Miles
0   25   50 KM

Build Your
Map Skills

Read a Historical Map

The Battle of Long Island was an early battle of the Revolutionary War. American forces under George Washington set up defensive positions around New York City. A large British force massed to the south on Long Island near Flatlands. From there, the British moved their troops so they would be in a position to attack.

While British troops held positions to the south and west of the American positions, another British force advanced on the Americans from the east through Jamaica Pass. This force wanted to get behind the Americans and cut them off from retreat. The British attacked. The outnumbered American troops were able to retreat in spite of the British attempt to cut them off.

The next day, the rain stopped the fighting. During the night of August 29–30, the Americans quietly moved their forces from Long Island to Manhattan. This unexpected move took the British completely by surprise. The Americans survived to fight another day. However, the British went on to capture New York City.

Refer to the battle map and answer the following questions.

1. Which of the two armies had the superior force?

   _____

2. Describe the three areas where the American troops were located at the beginning of the battle.

   _____

   _____

3. Name the British commanders involved in the battle.

_____

_____

4. Name the American commanders.

_____

_____

5. What were the British troops approaching from the east trying to accomplish?

_____

_____

6. How was the British victory incomplete?

_____

_____

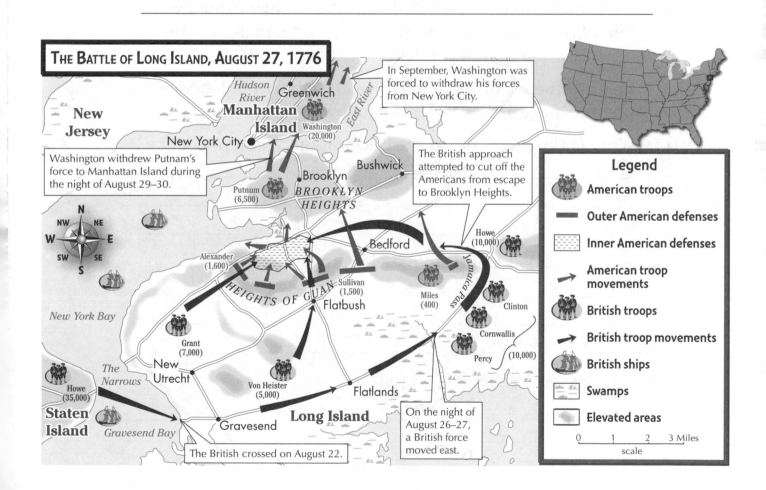

THE BATTLE OF LONG ISLAND, AUGUST 27, 1776

In September, Washington was forced to withdraw his forces from New York City.

Washington withdrew Putnam's force to Manhattan Island during the night of August 29–30.

The British approach attempted to cut off the Americans from escape to Brooklyn Heights.

On the night of August 26–27, a British force moved east.

The British crossed on August 22.

Legend
- American troops
- Outer American defenses
- Inner American defenses
- American troop movements
- British troops
- British troop movements
- British ships
- Swamps
- Elevated areas

0   1   2   3 Miles
scale

Learn about Cultural History

 How has history influenced the place where you live?

Americans are united by their cultural history. This includes the common experiences and beliefs that we share. Did you know that many of the beliefs we share today came from the time of the Revolutionary War? Some of them are expressed in the Declaration of Independence written in 1776.

Refer to the excerpts from the Declaration of Independence on Appendix page 101. Answer the following questions.

1. What is the Preamble to the Declaration of Independence?

   _____

   _____

   _____

2. What are "inalienable rights"? List some of them.

   _____

   _____

   _____

3. Why are governments created?

   _____

   _____

   _____

4. What is the proper way to form a government?

_____

_____

_____

5. What do the people have the right to do if the government does not protect and respect their rights?

_____

_____

_____

6. Describe three grievances in the Declaration of Independence.

_____

_____

_____

_____

Think about the history of your region of the United States. Do some research to learn about a person or event that is part of your cultural history. Below are ways to get some ideas.

7. Find out if there is a festival in your community or state that celebrates the memory of an important event. If so, find out the story behind this celebration and write it in the space below or on a separate piece of paper.

_____

_____

_____

8. Find landmarks in your town. They may be historic buildings, parks, memorials, battle sites, or historic forts or settlements. What is the story behind the landmarks? Write it in the space below or on a separate piece of paper.

_____

_____

_____

The Region of the Great Lakes

The states of Ohio, Wisconsin, Michigan, Illinois, and Indiana share an important resource: the Great Lakes. These five lakes (Huron, Ontario, Michigan, Erie, and Superior) serve as a transportation route, a recreational resource, and a source of fresh water. (See page Appendix page 102 for more information about the Great Lakes.)

The Great Lakes region is mostly level, with some gently rolling hills. Rugged country can be found in southeastern Ohio, southern Indiana and Illinois, and southwestern Wisconsin. Northern Michigan and Wisconsin are home to large forests. Regional waterways include the Mississippi and Ohio rivers.

In the mid-1800s, the Great Lakes region became one of the greatest industrial areas of the world. Industrial cities like Chicago, Illinois, relied on new immigrants to work in factories. Lake freighters transported materials such as iron ore, coal, and lumber to manufacturing cities to make products such as steel, paper, and automobiles. Heavy manufacturing is still important to the Great Lakes region, though it has declined since the 1970s.

Recreation on the Great Lakes is important to the economy.

Agriculture has always been important. The soil is fertile and the region gets plenty of rain. Great Lakes farms produce corn, soybeans, alfalfa, hay, and fruits, such as apples and cherries. Hogs are plentiful in Illinois. Southern Wisconsin is especially famous for its milk, cheese, and butter production.

Boating and tourism are major industries on the Great Lakes today. Sport and commercial fishing bring $4 billion to the region each year. The area also has almost 600 state parks which get more than 250 million visitors every year.

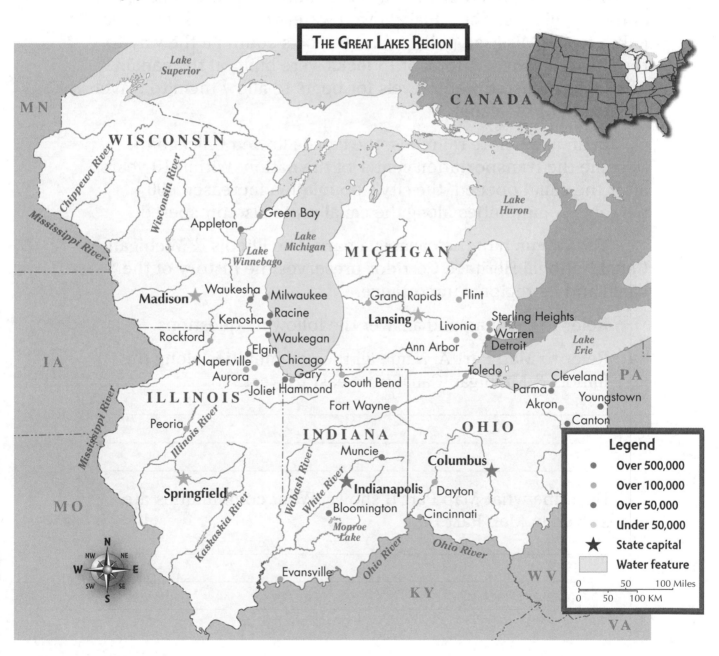

THE GREAT LAKES REGION

Legend
- Over 500,000
- Over 100,000
- Over 50,000
- Under 50,000
★ State capital
Water feature

Build Your
Map Skills

Compare Maps with Different Scales

A **canal** is a human-made waterway. The Illinois & Michigan Canal was completed in 1848. It ran 97 miles between Chicago and Peru, Illinois. The canal allowed water travel from the Great Lakes to the Mississippi River and to ports south all the way to the Gulf of Mexico. A total of 15 **locks** were built on the canal. The locks adjusted water levels for boats to allow them to travel the length of the canal.

In an age before railroads, the canal allowed Chicago to become the transportation center of the nation. Within 10 years after the canal opened, the city's population increased 600 percent. Communities along the canal route also prospered.

Today, much of the canal is a park. The Illinois & Michigan Canal National Heritage Corridor preserves the history of the canal and its regional importance.

Refer to the map and answer the following questions.

1. Refer to Map Part A. Name all the communities along the Illinois & Michigan Canal from east to west.

   _____

   _____

   _____

2. Describe what Map Part B shows. What communities are shown in Map Part B?

   _____

   _____

   _____

3. Name three things in Map Part B that are not shown in Map Part A.

_____

_____

_____

4. Name three things Map Part A shows that Map Part B does not show.

_____

_____

_____

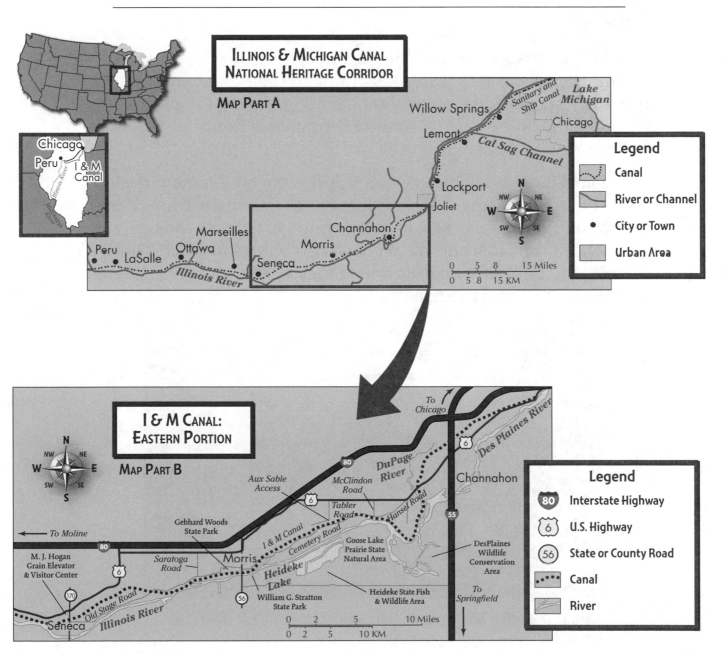

Canals of the Great Lakes

How have natural land or water features near you been changed for human use?

In this lesson, you learned how people of the Great Lakes region used the area's waterways to build their communities into great transportation centers. You have also learned that they changed the landscape by constructing canals to make transportation easier.

The Illinois & Michigan Canal was not the only transportation canal built in the Great Lakes region. For example, the Ohio & Erie Canal and the Miami & Erie Canal operated in Ohio. In Indiana, the Wabash & Erie Canal and the Whitewater Canal were built. The people who built these canals hoped they would become important to the commerce of the region.

Canals, like this one in Ohio, allowed goods to be shipped from the Midwest to eastern cities.

Select one of the canals mentioned in the passage above. Then, do some library research to complete the table below.

1. Name of canal: _____

2. Dates of construction: _____

3. What was the purpose of the canal? What waterways did it link together?

   _____

   _____

   _____

4. What products were shipped on the canal?

   _____

   _____

   _____

5. Did the canal affect economic growth? How?

   _____

   _____

   _____

6. Is the canal still in use? If so, how is it used today?

   _____

   _____

   _____

7. After you have completed the table, draw a map of the canal you chose on a separate piece of paper. Use the map of the Illinois & Michigan Canal on page 35 as a guide. Below are some guidelines:

   • If possible, draw the entire length of the canal.

   • Label the communities located along the canal.

   • Identify important waterways that the canal links together.

   • Include a map legend and a compass rose.

Jewels of the Lakes

The shoreline of the Great Lakes states includes a number of interesting landforms and **water forms. Peninsulas** and **islands** are plentiful. In fact, there are over 30,000 islands on the Great Lakes! That makes the region the world's largest freshwater island system. Water forms also include **rivers, lakes, channels, straits, bays,** and **coves.**

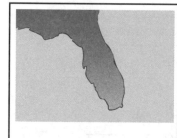

peninsula
Land with water on three sides that extends into a body of water such as a lake or ocean

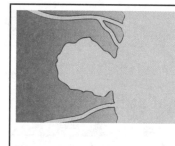

cove
A small, usually dish-shaped inlet that is smaller than a bay

island
Land that is surrounded by water on all sides

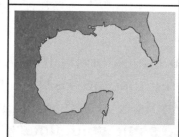

bay
A large inlet that is set off from a larger water body by points of land

river
A large, natural stream of water that is larger than a creek

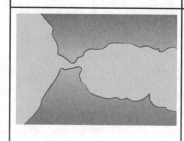

channel or strait
A narrow body of water between two points of land

Ecology is the relationship among plants, animals, and their surroundings. An **ecosystem** is a group of creatures living together in an environment. Islands are beautiful areas that are very important to the ecology of the Great Lakes region.

The lakes hold about 20 percent of the world's fresh water and support an incredible number of plants and animals. Some of these are threatened or **endangered.** Many people are working hard to protect these precious areas from pollution and other damage.

Lake Superior is the largest and most northern of the five Great Lakes. It contains Isle Royale and the Apostle Islands. The islands of the Great Lakes often have special issues in regard to their ecology. They tend to be home to many endangered animals and plants. In fact, many rare plants live only on Great Lakes islands.

The islands also provide places for fish to spawn (breed), waterfowl to nest, and migratory birds to rest. Protecting the islands of the Great Lakes is an important part of preserving the ecological variety of the entire Great Lakes region.

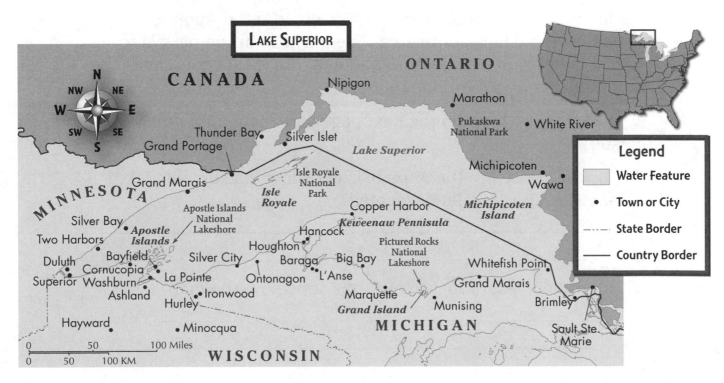

Build Your
Map Skills

Identify Landforms and Water Forms

According to their own history, the Chippewa were the first people to live in the Apostle Islands region. Their main home was Madeline Island, but they used resources from all of the islands. They fished year-round. They also used sugar from the abundant maple trees and gathered plants, such as leeks, fiddleheads, berries, and wintergreen, for both food and medicine. Bark from the white birch tree was used to make wigwams and canoes.

Beginning in the 1800s, the U.S. government began establishing areas called *reservations* for the Chippewa. In 1854, the final treaty between the Chippewa and the U.S. government created the Red Cliff Indian Reservation. Today, almost 1,000 people, mostly Native Americans, live on the reservation.

In 1970, the National Park Service created the Apostle Islands National Lakeshore area. The purpose of the park is to protect the region's wilderness and help the local economy of the Chippewa by promoting tourism.

Refer to the map on the next page and answer the following questions.

1. In what state are the Apostle Islands located? In what lake are the Apostle Islands located?

   _____

   _____

2. Identify at least four water forms shown on the map.

   _____

   _____

3. Identify at least two landforms shown on the map.

_____

_____

4. Which bays border the Red Cliff Indian Reservation? What points are included in it?

_____

_____

5. What two towns are located on the Bayfield Peninsula? Which one of these allows access to the islands?

_____

_____

_____

6. Which islands have lighthouses?

_____

_____

_____

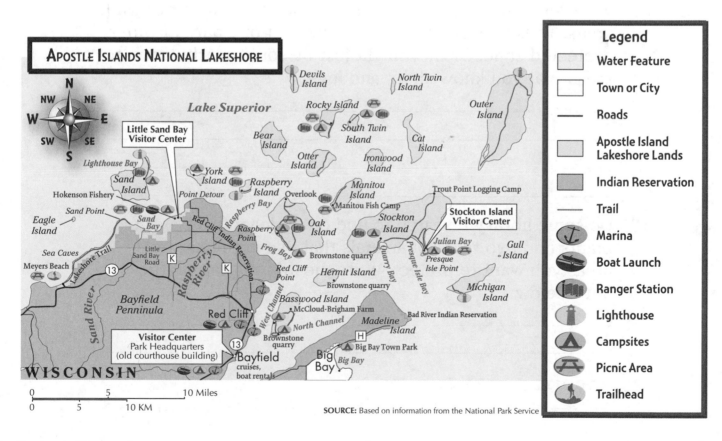

Preserve the Natural Areas

Something to Think About

What natural areas near your home are worth preserving?

In this lesson, you have learned about some natural areas that people want to protect. Now, think about the part of the country where you live. Are there any natural areas nearby that you think are worth preserving?

1. Write down at least three natural areas in your community, state, or region that you would like to see maintained for the future. These might be natural features such as rivers, waterfalls, islands, forests, deserts, meadows, or other wild areas. These areas might already be part of a park or other protected zone. Or they might just be some nearby natural areas that you know about and love.

_____

_____

_____

_____

2. Do some library research to find out at least two types of plants and two types of animals that live in the natural areas you want to protect. Write the information on the lines below.

_____

_____

_____

_____

3. If these areas are not protected, what do you think might happen to them? Use the lines below to describe how they might become endangered over time.

_____

_____

_____

_____

_____

_____

4. Ask at least three adults if they know about the areas you want to protect. What do these areas mean to them? Do they agree that the areas should be protected? Why or why not? Write what you find out on the lines below.

_____

_____

_____

_____

_____

_____

5. Now that you have collected some information, write a paragraph describing why the natural areas are worth preserving.

_____

_____

_____

_____

_____

_____

The Region of the Upper Plains

The Upper Plains region is a huge area of the north-central United States. North and South Dakota, Nebraska, Kansas, Minnesota, Iowa, and Missouri are included in this area. The region is bounded by the Rocky Mountains to the west, Canada to the north, and the Mississippi River to the east. It includes much flat prairie. However, there are many other kinds of land and water forms, including South Dakota's Black Hills, Minnesota's lakes, and the Ozark region of Missouri.

In the early 1800s, European settlers thought of the Plains as a harsh and undesirable place to live because there were few trees for building homes and a limited supply of water. Because of the settlers heading west on their way to the Pacific coast, Missouri got the nickname "Gateway to the West."

The Upper Plains is America's top wheat-producing region.

In 1862, the United States government offered to give 160 acres of land to any family that moved to the Plains and lived on the land for at least five years. The Plains eventually became home to large numbers of immigrants from Norway and Sweden, as well as others from Germany, Ireland, and Russia.

The Upper Plains is America's top wheat-producing region. Other important grain crops include sorghum, barley, and rye. Ranching has always been important to the region. Kansas is America's second-leading producer of beef. Hog production is important in Iowa and Missouri. In Minnesota and Missouri, food processing, chemicals, and light manufacturing are important. In addition, the Mississippi River has helped large cities in Minnesota, Iowa, and Missouri to become leading transportation centers.

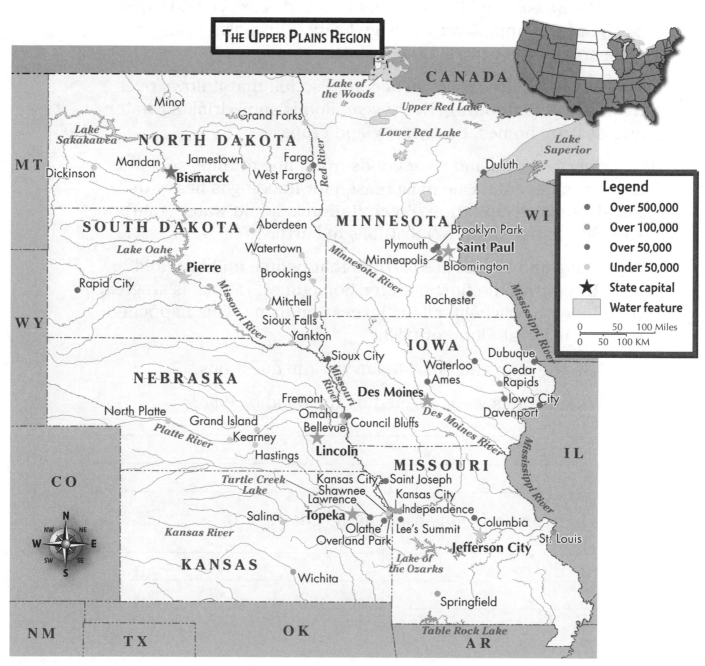

THE UPPER PLAINS REGION

Legend
- Over 500,000
- Over 100,000
- Over 50,000
- Under 50,000
- ★ State capital
- Water feature

Build Your

Map Skills

Understand the Great Flood of 1993

The Mississippi River and its tributaries are considered to be the Mississippi River drainage **basin.** This basin drains a wide area of the central United States.

When a river or stream becomes so full that it flows over its banks, it is **flooding.** Every year, floods spoil drinking water and destroy homes, businesses, and crops.

Every stream and river floods from time to time, so floods are natural events. One main reason for flooding is heavy or long-lasting precipitation. **Precipitation** is liquid water (rain) or solid water (ice or snow) that falls to Earth.

Dams and **levees** are barriers that people build to hold back or control the flow of water. Sometimes, rainfall is so great that floods overwhelm all the levees and dams. This happened during the Great Flood of 1993.

Use the map and chart to answer the questions.

1. Which states were affected by the flood of 1993?

   _____

   _____

   _____

2. What comparison is made in the chart?

   _____

   _____

   _____

3. How much rain does the region usually receive in June? How much actually fell in June of 1993?

_____

_____

_____

4. Approximately how much precipitation actually fell in the region from January to August 1993? Approximately how much falls during these months in a normal year?

_____

_____

_____

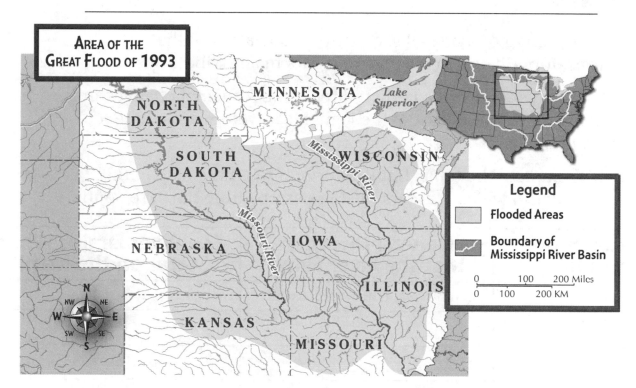

AREA OF THE GREAT FLOOD OF 1993

MINNESOTA

Lake Superior

NORTH DAKOTA

SOUTH DAKOTA

WISCONSIN

Mississippi River

Missouri River

NEBRASKA

IOWA

ILLINOIS

KANSAS

MISSOURI

Legend

Flooded Areas

Boundary of Mississippi River Basin

0   100   200 Miles
0   100   200 KM

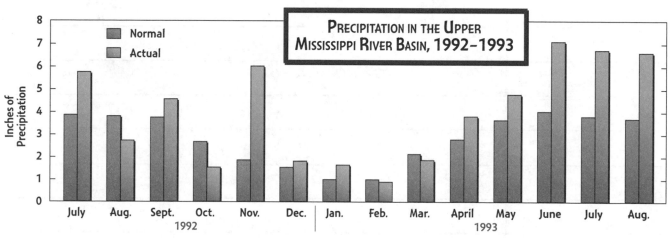

PRECIPITATION IN THE UPPER MISSISSIPPI RIVER BASIN, 1992–1993

Normal

Actual

Inches of Precipitation

July   Aug.   Sept.   Oct.   Nov.   Dec. | Jan.   Feb.   Mar.   April   May   June   July   Aug.

1992   1993

Learn about Tributaries

Something to Think About

How do tributaries create a river system?

The map on page 49 shows the headwaters of the Mississippi River along with some if its major tributaries.

All rivers flow in a certain direction because of changes in **elevation,** or the height of the land. **Headwaters** are where a stream begins.

1. Complete the table. List each tributary on the map in the order in which it enters the Mississippi, from north to south.

Name of Tributary	General Direction that the River Flows	The River Drains What States on the Map?
Minnesota River	southeast, then northeast	Minnesota, South Dakota

2. What lake is at the Mississippi headwaters?

_____

Pick one of the tributaries shown on the map and do library research to learn more about it.

3. What is the name of the river you have selected?

_____

4. Where does it begin? Where does it end?

_____

_____

5. Name some communities located along the tributary.

_____

_____

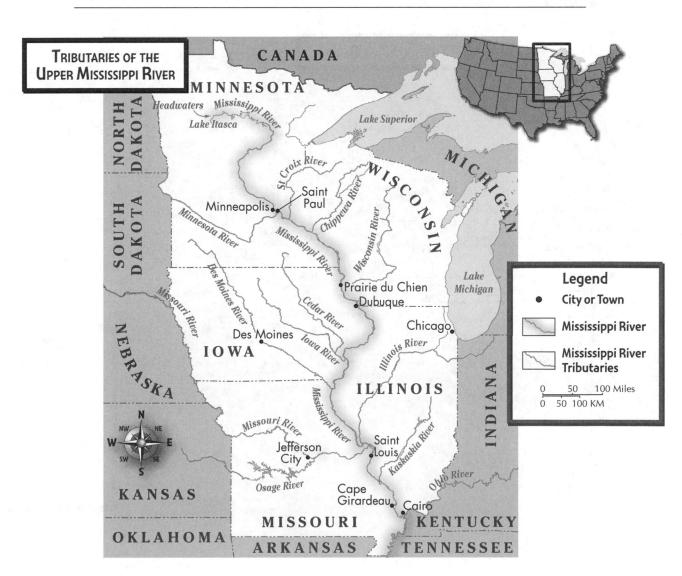

The Southeast Region

The Southeast region of the United States is bordered on the east by the Atlantic Ocean and on the south by the Gulf of Mexico. Within this region, the Appalachian Mountains extend from West Virginia into northern Georgia.

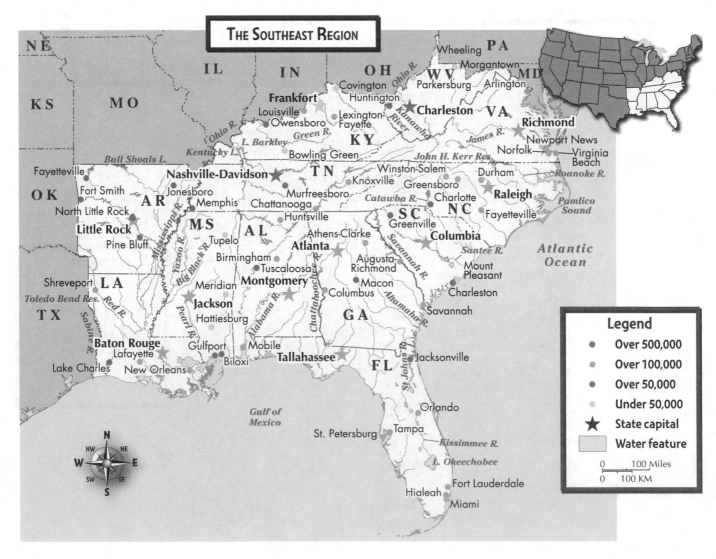

THE SOUTHEAST REGION

Legend
- ● Over 500,000
- ● Over 100,000
- ● Over 50,000
- ● Under 50,000
- ★ State capital
- ▢ Water feature

0   100 Miles
0   100 KM

Many important leaders of the American Revolution were southerners, and four of America's first five presidents came from Virginia. Shortly after the Revolution, the southern economy began to focus almost completely on agriculture. This was in contrast to the northern states, where manufacturing began to take on greater importance. Large numbers of enslaved Africans were brought into the South to work on the **plantations.** In the 1860s, conflict over **slavery** caused a split between the North and the South that resulted in the Civil War.

Today, the Southeast region has a diverse economy and is an important manufacturing region. The Mississippi River and its tributaries are major transportation routes.

Numerous oil and natural gas wells are found in the Gulf of Mexico. Coal mining is important in West Virginia and Kentucky. Regional agricultural products include soybeans, corn, citrus fruits, beef cattle, poultry, rice, and peanuts, cotton, and tobacco. Tourism is strong in many parts of the region, such as the mountains of Tennessee and the beaches of Virginia, the Carolinas, and Florida.

Temperate, tropical, and even some arid areas can be found in the Southeast region. (See Lesson 1 for more information on climate zones.) **Wetlands,** including **swamps,** and small, slow-moving streams called **bayous** are common environments in the southernmost parts of the Southeast region. Violent tropical storms called **hurricanes** threaten people and property during certain seasons of the year along the Gulf and Atlantic coasts.

Wetlands are common in the Deep South.

Build Your
Map Skills

Understand a Natural Disaster

During the months of late summer and fall, hurricanes pose a threat to many people who live along the southeast coast from Texas to North Carolina.

Hurricanes gather heat and energy from the warm waters of the Atlantic Ocean and Gulf of Mexico. The storms move in a counterclockwise direction around an "eye," which is a calm center area 20 to 30 miles wide. The storm may extend as much as 400 miles from the eye.

Hurricanes have winds of at least 74 miles per hour. When they come onto land, the heavy rain, violent winds, and high waves can cause major destruction. Communities where hurricanes are likely to strike must develop plans for dealing with such storms.

In August 2005, a very big hurricane named Katrina hit the southeast coast along the Gulf of Mexico. Florida, Mississippi, Alabama, and Louisiana suffered major destruction. Many communities were flooded. More than 1,400 people were killed and another 1.5 million people had to leave their damaged homes.

Refer to the map and answer the following questions.

1. The map shows parts of which states?

_____

_____

2. Which state did Katrina touch first when it hit land?

_____

3. Use landmarks to describe where Katrina struck land and the direction it traveled.

_____

_____

_____

4. Which areas on the map had the most catastrophic damage? Name the county or parish and state.

_____

_____

_____

5. Which areas experienced the worst flooding?

_____

_____

_____

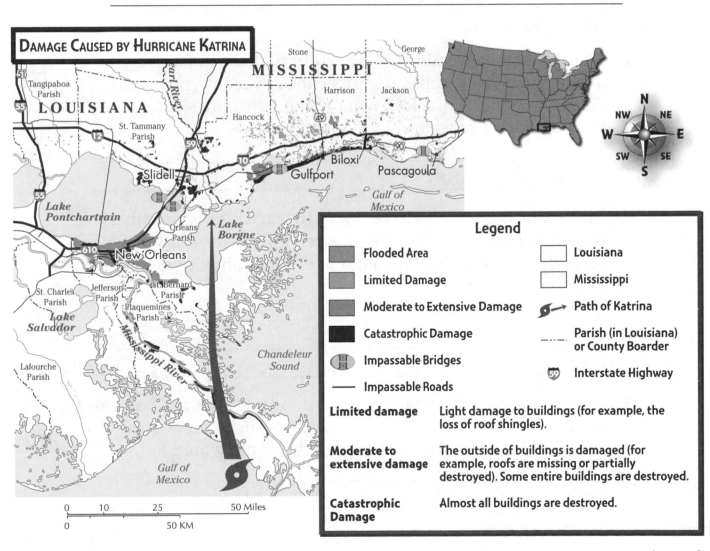

DAMAGE CAUSED BY HURRICANE KATRINA

Legend

Flooded Area	Louisiana
Limited Damage	Mississippi
Moderate to Extensive Damage	Path of Katrina
Catastrophic Damage	Parish (in Louisiana) or County Boarder
Impassable Bridges	Interstate Highway
Impassable Roads	

Limited damage — Light damage to buildings (for example, the loss of roof shingles).

Moderate to extensive damage — The outside of buildings is damaged (for example, roofs are missing or partially destroyed). Some entire buildings are destroyed.

Catastrophic Damage — Almost all buildings are destroyed.

Prepare a Disaster Plan

Something to **Think** About

How can a disaster plan help your family?

More than likely, your home will not be affected by a natural disaster. But in case a disaster does strike, you would be smart to create a plan to deal with it. Appendix page 103 presents a few ideas.

1. Start by listing the kinds of disasters that are most likely to affect you. For example, do hurricanes ever hit your area? Tornadoes? Earthquakes? What about lightning strikes, flooding, or heavy snow?

    _____

    _____

2. Does your community have a way to warn you of possible problems? For example, does a siren go off to warn you of tornadoes? What does it sound like? What should you do when you hear it?

    _____

    _____

    _____

3. For some types of disasters, like tornadoes, it might be best to stay in your home. For these kinds of disasters, write exactly where the safest place in your home would be.

    _____

    _____

4. For other types of disasters, like fires, you need to get out of the house right away. Plan at least two escape routes.

_____

_____

_____

_____

5. In the space below, describe a place where your family can meet if you have to leave your home because of a disaster. List the address and phone number of this location.

_____

_____

_____

_____

6. What will you do with your pets if disaster strikes? Think about it and write your plan below.

_____

_____

_____

_____

_____

Consider all your family members, including pets, when you develop a disaster plan.

7. Is there anything you can do to keep your home safe before disaster hits? Are there any special supplies you should keep on hand? How might you protect valuable items?

_____

_____

_____

8. After you have put together your plan, call a family meeting and discuss your ideas with everyone. Explain why it's important to have a disaster plan. Listen to everyone's ideas and suggestions. Then, prepare a finished plan on a separate piece of paper. Review the plan every few months so everyone remembers what to do.

Battles of the Civil War

A **civil war** is a war between groups of people who belong to the same country. The American Civil War was fought between a group of northern and western states (the Union) and a group of southern states (the Confederacy). The war began when the southern states left the United States to establish their own country mainly to preserve slavery. They called their country the *Confederate States of America*.

The Civil War happened for many reasons. Through the early 1800s, the culture and economy of the North and South was very different. There were more large cities in the North than in the South. There also were more factories there. The economy of the South was very dependent upon agriculture and slavery.

In the 1830s, a strong **abolition movement** began in the North. Abolitionists believed that slavery was against the ideals upon which the country was founded. They wanted to abolish it. Through the mid-1800s, the South became threatened by the addition of new western states to the Union. If the new states became free states, that could tip the balance of power in Congress in favor of anti-slavery forces in the North.

Abraham Lincoln was elected president of the United States in 1860. At this time, the conflict between the North and South reached a crisis. Lincoln had promised to keep the United States together. Though not an abolitionist, Lincoln opposed the spread of slavery into the western territories or in new states. Fearing the loss of their political power, a group of southern states **seceded,** or left the Union, and formed the Confederate States of America. Some states that permitted slavery did not leave the Union. They were called *Union Slave States* or *Border States*.

On April 12, 1861, Confederate troops attacked Fort Sumter, South Carolina, which was occupied by Union troops. The Civil War had begun. Before it would end four years later, many thousands of Americans would be killed. Most of the battles took place in the South. It took many decades for the region to recover from the war.

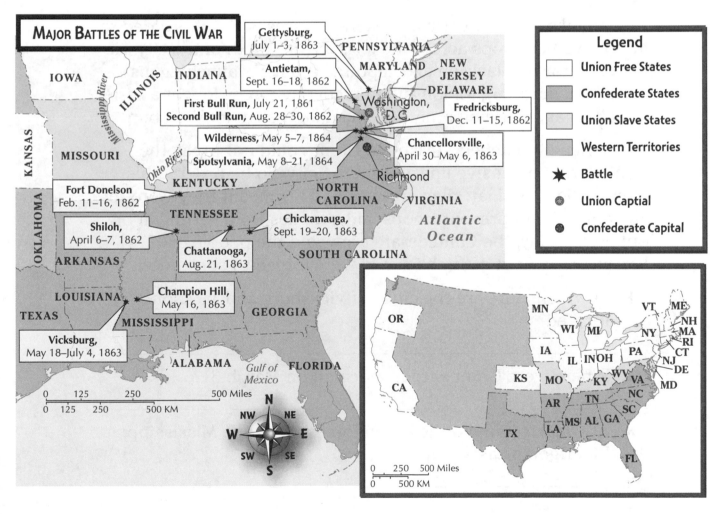

Build Your
Map Skills

Read a Battlefield Map

At the beginning of the Civil War, the Confederacy controlled the southern portion of the Mississippi River. Southerners used the river to get supplies and fresh troops to Confederate forces. If the Union could get control of the Mississippi, it could split the Confederacy in two. Vicksburg was a key city on the Mississippi. It sat on high cliffs overlooking the river. From there, the Confederate army could control the river by firing down on Union ships.

To take Vicksburg, Union general Ulysses S. Grant decided to first move his troops across the Mississippi, south of the city. He marched toward Jackson and captured it before launching his attack on Vicksburg. Union and Confederate forces fought a series of battles as the Union army advanced on the city of Vicksburg.

When he reached Vicksburg, Grant could not break the Confederate defensive line around the city. So he ordered his men to dig in and lay **siege** to the city. This meant they were to surround it and prevent troops and supplies from getting in or out. Eventually, the Confederate army and the people of Vicksburg ran out of supplies and were forced to surrender.

1. In which state are the cities of Vicksburg and Jackson located?

   _____

2. Where were Grant's troops located on March 31?

   _____

3. At which town did the Union forces cross the Mississippi River going east?

   _____

4. About how long did it take Grant's troops to get from Port Gibson to Jackson?

_____

5. Which two important rail lines crossed at the town of Jackson?

_____

_____

6. From Jackson, which direction did Grant's troops turn to head toward Vicksburg? Which river did they cross on their way to the city?

_____

_____

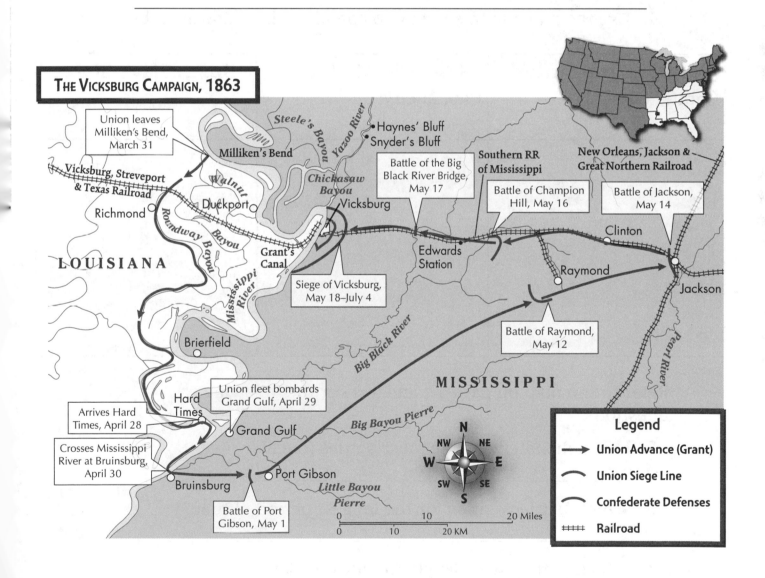

THE VICKSBURG CAMPAIGN, 1863

Union leaves Milliken's Bend, March 31

Steele's Bayou

Yazoo River

Haynes' Bluff
Snyder's Bluff

Milliken's Bend

Southern RR of Mississippi

New Orleans, Jackson & Great Northern Railroad

Vicksburg, Streveport & Texas Railroad

Walnut Bayou

Chickasaw Bayou

Battle of the Big Black River Bridge, May 17

Battle of Champion Hill, May 16

Battle of Jackson, May 14

Duckport

Vicksburg

Richmond

Roundway Bayou

Grant's Canal

Edwards Station

Clinton

LOUISIANA

Mississippi River

Siege of Vicksburg, May 18–July 4

Raymond

Jackson

Big Black River

Battle of Raymond, May 12

Brierfield

MISSISSIPPI

Pearl River

Union fleet bombards Grand Gulf, April 29

Hard Times

Arrives Hard Times, April 28

Grand Gulf

Big Bayou Pierre

N
NW NE
W E
SW SE
S

Crosses Mississippi River at Bruinsburg, April 30

Port Gibson

Bruinsburg

Little Bayou Pierre

Battle of Port Gibson, May 1

0   10   20 Miles
0   10   20 KM

Legend

→ Union Advance (Grant)

⌒ Union Siege Line

⌒ Confederate Defenses

++++ Railroad

Make a Civil War Time Line

 How can a time line help you to organize events?

1. Use the maps in this lesson to complete the following table.

Union Free States Capital city:	Confederate States Capital city:	Union Slave States

Refer to the map on page 57, and answer the following questions.

2. In which state were the most battles fought?

_____

3. Which battle went on for the longest period of time?

_____

4. Which battles were fought in only one day?

_____

5. A **time line** can help to organize key historical events over a period of time. Time lines show events in **chronological order** (in the order the events happened). Use the map on page 57 to make a time line for important Civil War battles. Record the information in the table below.

Name of Battle	Date of Battle (from first to last)	State Where Battle Was Fought

6. Select one of the battles listed in the time line above, and do some library research to learn more about it. Write two or three paragraphs about the battle on a separate piece of paper. Be sure to answer the following questions:

   • When and where did the battle occur?

   • Who were the leading generals?

   • Why was the battle important?

   • How many soldiers lost their lives in the battle?

   • How many soldiers were wounded?

   • Was the battle a clear victory for the Union or for the Confederacy? If neither, explain.

The Southwest Region

The four states of the Southwest region—Oklahoma, Texas, New Mexico, and Arizona—are among our nation's largest. The climate and landforms of the region are varied and often surprising. More than half of Arizona features mountains and **plateaus** (high, flat lands). Parts of the Mojave and Sonoran **deserts** are also in Arizona.

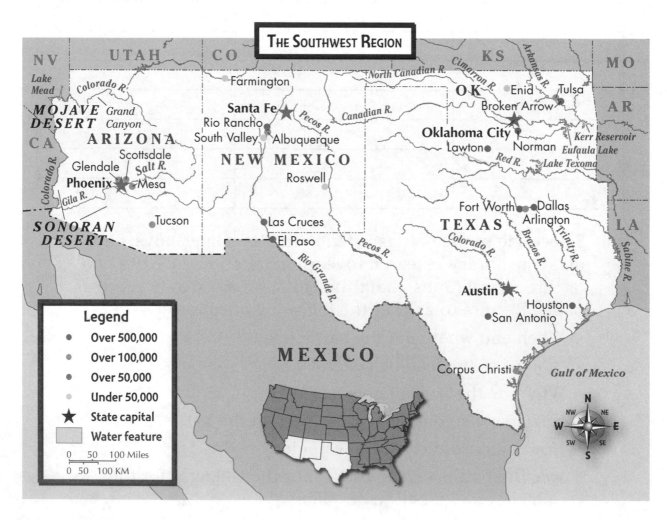

THE SOUTHWEST REGION

Legend
- Over 500,000
- Over 100,000
- Over 50,000
- Under 50,000
- ★ State capital
- Water feature

0 50 100 Miles
0 50 100 KM

Landforms in New Mexico include deserts, mesas, and mountain peaks. **Mesas** are high areas of land with flat tops and sides that are usually steep cliffs. The state features a large area of forested mountains. The central part of the state is divided almost in two by the Rio Grande River.

Texas has low coastal areas near the Gulf of Mexico, plains in the north, and hill country in between. The wetter eastern part of Oklahoma is forested, but the western part of the state is mostly semi-arid plains.

The climate varies greatly throughout the region. Annual rainfall is greater toward the east. The drier regions mostly support beef cattle and sheep. Poultry is important to the Oklahoma economy. Wheat and cotton are grown in Texas and Oklahoma.

The energy industry is very important to the economy of the Southwest. Texas and Oklahoma are major producers of oil and natural gas. Mining is important in New Mexico and Arizona. Income from tourism, especially in the Grand Canyon area, is also important.

The influence of Hispanic and Native American culture is strong throughout the region. The population in the Southwest is growing rapidly, partly due to the warm climate.

Plateaus and mesas are just two of the varied landforms of the Southwest.

Build Your
Map Skills

Learn about Coronado and the Cities of Gold

Conquistadors were the Spanish soldiers and explorers who conquered much of North and South America for Spain. Francisco Vásquez de Coronado was a Spanish conquistador who lived in Mexico almost 500 years ago.

In 1540, Coronado heard stories about seven great cities made of gold. In February 1540, he set out on an expedition from Mexico to find these cities.

By July, Coronado reached the location of the first "golden city," Háwikuh. But instead of gold, he found only a **pueblo,** or settlement of Indians. The conquistadors were bitterly disappointed.

While at Háwikuh, Coronado sent one of his captains, Garcia López de Cárdenas, to explore the region to the northwest. After about 20 days, Cárdenas and his search party came upon the Grand Canyon and the Colorado River. They were probably the first Europeans to see the Grand Canyon. Another captain, Hernando de Alvarado, explored to the east. At Cicúye, Alvarado met "the Turk," a Native American who described a rich country toward the northeast, called *Quivira.*

"The Turk" convinced Coronado to continue his **expedition** to Quivira the next spring. After a long journey, Coronado found that the Quivira Indians had no gold. "The Turk" had made up the story so the conquistadors would become lost. After learning the truth, Coronado and his group made their way back to Mexico in shame due to their failure.

Refer to the map and answer the following questions.

1. Coronado traveled through which present-day states within the United States?

_____

2. Coronado traveled through the lands of what Native American tribes? Name three of them.

_____

3. About how far did Cárdenas travel from Háwikuh on his journey to the Grand Canyon?

_____

4. Name at least four rivers Coronado's party crossed.

_____

_____

5. According to "the Turk," in which present-day state was Quivira, the "city of gold"?

_____

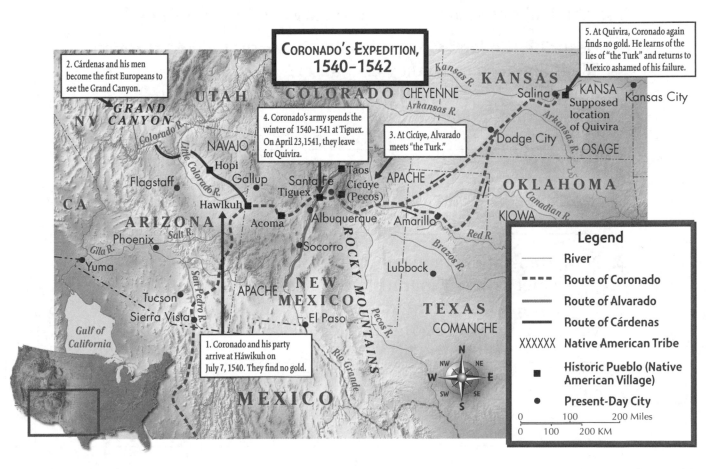

Write a Journal Based on a Map

How can a map tell a story?

The map of Coronado's expedition on page 65 tells part of the story of his travels. Several important things that happened during the expedition are noted on the map. This helps you follow Coronado's movements throughout the region.

In this activity, you will think about what it might have been like for Coronado and his men on each stage of their expedition. First, think about some things Coronado and his party saw.

1. Describe the land Coronado and his party traveled through. What landforms did they encounter? What climate did they find there? Reread pages 62–63 for some clues. Write your answer on the lines below.

   _____

   _____

   _____

   _____

2. Now, think about some of the people Coronado and his party met on their journey. Do some research in the library to find out how Native Americans in that region lived. Write what you find out on the lines below.

   _____

   _____

   _____

   _____

3. Assume that you are traveling with Coronado. Use the information you gathered to write a journal about your adventures. Use the map and description of the expedition on pages 64–65 for reference. Below are some points you may want to address in your journal.

- What was the long journey like through the desert wilderness of Mexico and Arizona to Háwikuh?

- How did you feel upon finding that Háwikuh was just a pueblo with no gold?

- What was the reaction of the Cárdenas party upon discovering the Grand Canyon of the Colorado River?

- Describe the expedition's renewed hope for riches after talking to "the Turk" about Quivira.

- Describe the long journey from Tiguex across the mountains to the plains of Kansas.

- What were your thoughts when you found that the Turk had lied about Quivira?

- How did you feel during your return trip to Mexico, knowing that your expedition had failed?

Write at least two paragraphs describing the expedition. Use the lines below for your journal entries.

_____

_____

_____

_____

_____

_____

_____

_____

_____

_____

The Rocky Mountain Region

The Rocky Mountain region consists of five large states: Idaho, Montana, Wyoming, Utah, and Colorado. The Rocky Mountains begin in Canada and extend south to end near Santa Fe, New Mexico. The **Continental Divide** is located along the length of the Rocky Mountains. To the east of the divide, rivers flow into the Mississippi River or into Hudson Bay in Canada. To the west of the divide, rivers flow into the Pacific.

Denver, Colorado, is the largest city in the region. It is a major business, industrial, and transportation center. Other important cities include Salt Lake City, Utah; Billings, Montana; Boise, Idaho; and Cheyenne, Wyoming.

Mining and tourism are important to the economy of the Rocky Mountain region. Lumber is also an important regional resource. The great natural beauty of the mountains draws large numbers of tourists to locations such as Pikes Peak, Yellowstone National Park, and Glacier National Park.

A calm river in the Rocky Mountains.

Agriculture is limited in many parts of the region because of poor soil or lack of rainfall. However, Idaho produces about one-third of the potatoes grown in the United States, as well as beets, wheat, and barley (which are also grown in other Rocky Mountain states). Ranching is important in the region, too, especially in Wyoming and Montana.

Native American culture is part of the shared heritage of this region. The mountains are home to many tribes, including the Apache, Blackfoot, Cheyenne, Shoshoni, and Nez Perce. In 1832, the first wagon train across the Rockies passed through Wyoming. By the late 1800s, white settlers and the discovery of gold in the region pushed Native Americans onto reservations and changed their way of life forever.

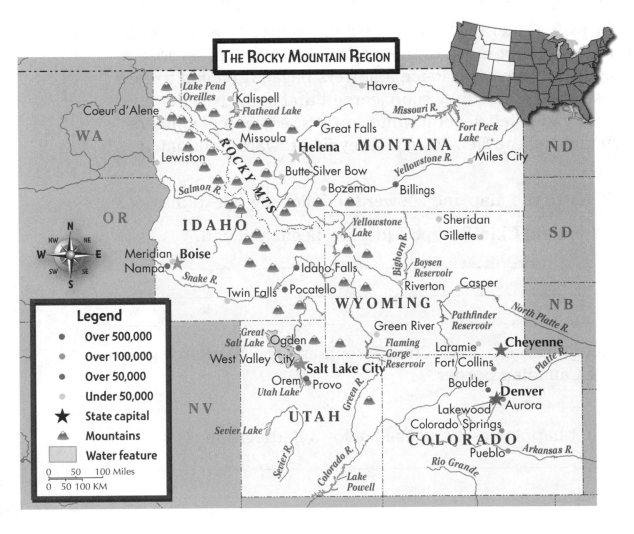

THE ROCKY MOUNTAIN REGION

Legend
- Over 500,000
- Over 100,000
- Over 50,000
- Under 50,000
★ State capital
▲ Mountains
  Water feature

0   50   100 Miles
0 50 100 KM

Build Your
Map Skills

Learn about the Nez Perce Trail

In the early 1800s, the lands of the Native American tribe called the *Nez Perce* spread through Idaho, Oregon, and Washington. In 1855, the tribe even worked with whites to create a reservation in the Wallowa Valley in parts of Oregon, Washington, and Idaho. But when gold was found on Nez Perce land in 1863, the U.S. government took millions of acres from the tribe and tried to force it onto a small reservation in Idaho.

In 1877, General Oliver Howard threatened to attack if the Nez Perce did not move to the Idaho reservation. Chief Joseph and a few hundred Nez Perce followers began traveling toward the reservation. But they soon learned that some Nez Perce warriors had killed several white settlers. A group of soldiers began chasing the Nez Perce as they fled toward freedom in Canada.

Refer to the map and answer the following questions.

1. Where did Chief Joseph's journey begin and end?

   _____

   _____

   _____

2. About how close did Chief Joseph and the Nez Perce get to the Canadian border?

   _____

3. What happened at Camas Meadows Battleground?

   _____

   _____

4. What happened at Bear's Paw Battleground?

_____

_____

5. Where did the army finally move Chief Joseph?

_____

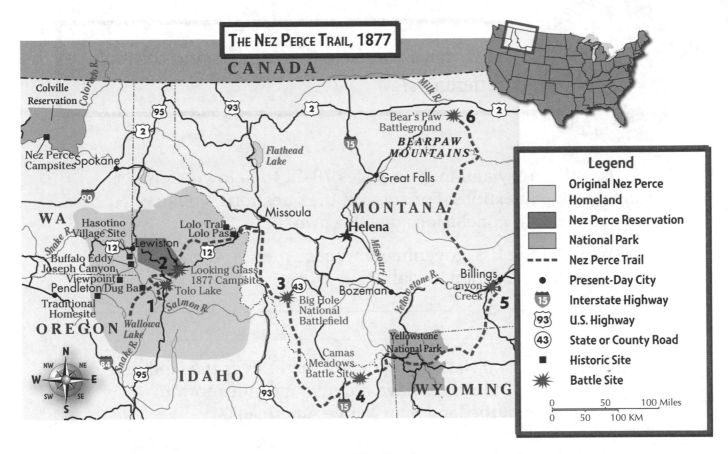

THE NEZ PERCE TRAIL, 1877

CANADA

Colville Reservation

Colorado R.

Nez Perce Campsites — Spokane

Flathead Lake

Bear's Paw Battleground **6**

Milk R.

BEARPAW MOUNTAINS

Great Falls

MONTANA

Helena

Missoula

WA

Hasotino Village Site
Lolo Trail
Lolo Pass

Snake R.

Lewiston

Buffalo Eddy
Joseph Canyon Viewpoint
Pendleton — Dug Bar
Traditional Homesite

2

Looking Glass 1877 Campsite
Tolo Lake

Salmon R.

1

Wallowa Lake

OREGON

Snake R.

IDAHO

3 (43)

Big Hole National Battlefield

Missouri R.

Bozeman

Yellowstone R.

Billings
Canyon Creek **5**

Camas Meadows Battle Site

Yellowstone National Park

4

WYOMING

N NE E SE S SW W NW

Legend

Original Nez Perce Homeland

Nez Perce Reservation

National Park

- - - Nez Perce Trail

● Present-Day City

(15) Interstate Highway

(93) U.S. Highway

(43) State or County Road

■ Historic Site

✳ Battle Site

0   50   100 Miles
0   50   100 KM

1: June 17: _Battle at White Bird Canyon._ The Nez Perce win a battle against a group of U.S. soldiers.

2: July 11–12: _Battle at Clearwater._ General Howard attacks the Nez Perce at the Battle of Clearwater. The Nez Perce withdraw.

3: August 9-10: _Battle at Big Hole._ The army launches a surprise attack on the Nez Perce camp, and the Nez Perce suffer many losses. The Nez Perce counterattack, overwhelm the soldiers, and then retreat.

4: August 20: _Battle at Camas Meadows._ The Nez Perce launch a surprise attack. The army loses most of its horses and mules and is defeated.

5: September 13: _Battle at Canyon Creek._ The army and Nez Perce fight a running battle with no clear winner. However, the Nez Perce lose many of their horses, and this later hurts their retreat.

6: September 30-October 5: _Battle at Bear's Paw._ The army attacks a Nez Perce camp and the Nez Perce are encircled. The battle lasts five days. Chief Joseph surrenders. About 200 Nez Perce are able to escape to Canada. The rest are taken to a reservation in Oklahoma. They are relocated to the Colville Reservation in 1885.

Understanding Cultural Differences

How can a map help us to understand cultural differences?

Use the story and map on pages 70–71 to help you answer the following questions. For some of the questions, you may have to come to conclusions on your own.

1. Why did the U.S. government want to put the Nez Perce on a small reservation in Idaho?

_____

_____

2. The whites and Native Americans fought over the land in this region. Did whites have different attitudes toward ownership of the land than Native Americans?

_____

_____

_____

_____

3. Why do you think that the United States honors the Nez Perce today through a historic trail even though these groups fought in 1877?

_____

_____

_____

_____

4. Why do you think Chief Joseph and his followers fled toward Canada after hearing that some Nez Perce had attacked white settlers?

_____

_____

5. Was Chief Joseph ever able to return to his homeland in the Wallowa Valley?

_____

_____

_____

_____

Now pick a research topic to learn more about Nez Perce history and culture. Choose one of the following topics (or think of one of your own) and do some library research. Write a paragraph about your topic on a separate piece of paper. Some projects may require you to do a sketch or draw a map.

- What did Nez Perce homes look like in the 1800s? How were they built?

- What foods did the Nez Perce eat? Describe how they were cooked and prepared.

- What games did the Nez Perce children play? Describe their favorite toys.

- Find out where most Nez Perce live today. Show some of these locations on a map you create.

- Describe and/or draw traditional Nez Perce clothing.

- Create a time line showing the important events in the life of Chief Joseph.

- Describe the kinds of tools the Nez Perce people used.

- Find out about the Nez Perce tribal flag. Create your own version and explain what it means.

- Learn how the Nez Perce got that name. Find out what they call themselves.

LESSON 13

The Region of the Far West

Washington, Oregon, Nevada, California, Alaska, and Hawaii are the Far West states. Early Native American tribes of Washington and Oregon include the Bannock, Chinook, and Nez Perce. The Inuit live in the Arctic regions of Alaska. Native Hawaiians have lived on the islands for 1,000 years.

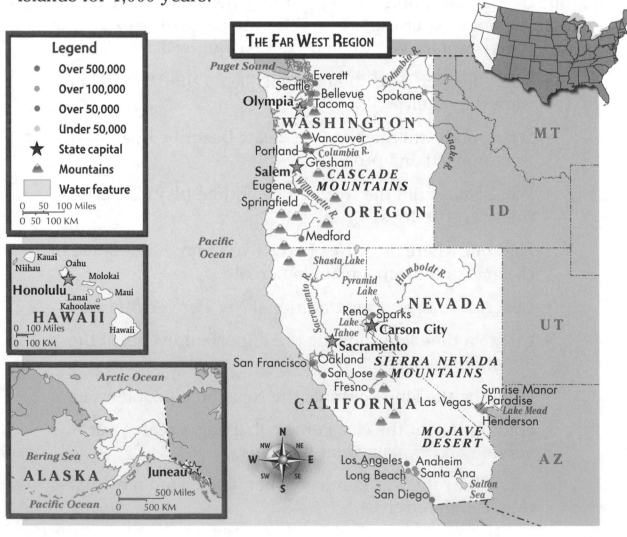

Europeans began exploring the Pacific coast in the mid-1500s. By the late 1700s, Spain had established a number of settlements in California. Major settlement of the region began in the 1840s. Gold was discovered in California in 1849, drawing thousands to the West.

The Far West region is strongly influenced by Asian, Native American, and Hispanic cultures. Los Angeles, California, is heavily influenced by its large Hispanic population. Other major cities in the region include San Diego and San Francisco in California; Seattle, Washington; Portland, Oregon; Honolulu, Hawaii; and Las Vegas, Nevada.

Agriculture is an important part of the Far West economy. California, Washington, and Oregon produce much of the nation's fruits and vegetables. Lumber is important to the economy of Washington and Oregon. The Far West is home to many high-tech companies, such as computer software developers and airplane designers. Tourism is also vital to the Far West. Las Vegas, Nevada, and southern California are major entertainment centers.

Great mountain ranges run along the Pacific Coast. East of these ranges are many fertile valleys, such as the San Joaquin in California and the Willamette in Oregon. Farther east lie still more mountains: the Cascade Range to the north and the Sierra Nevada Range in the south.

The beautiful Cascade Range runs through Washington and Oregon.

Build Your
Map Skills

Read a Map to Learn about a Natural Event

The Cascade Range of the northwestern United Sates is volcanic. A **volcano** is a mountain where **magma** (hot, liquefied rock) can erupt through Earth's surface. (Refer to Appendix page 105 to learn more about volcanoes.)

Early on May 18, 1980, Mount St. Helens in Washington State erupted (exploded violently). The power of the blast was enormous. Many square miles of forest were blown down or buried under ashes and rocks. Thousands of animals were killed. Creeks and rivers were clogged with trees and mud. The eruption killed 57 people and destroyed 200 homes.

It's hard to believe, but plant and animal life has returned to the area. By now, more than 25 years later, much of the area is green again.

Use the maps to answer the following questions.

1. Name three communities on the map that may have been in danger during the Mount St. Helens eruption.

   _____

2. Name two lakes located within the Mount St. Helens Monument.

   _____

3. Describe the location of monument headquarters.

   _____

4. In one sentence, describe what Map 2 shows.

_____

_____

5. What rivers and creeks were mostly destroyed as a result of the eruption?

_____

_____

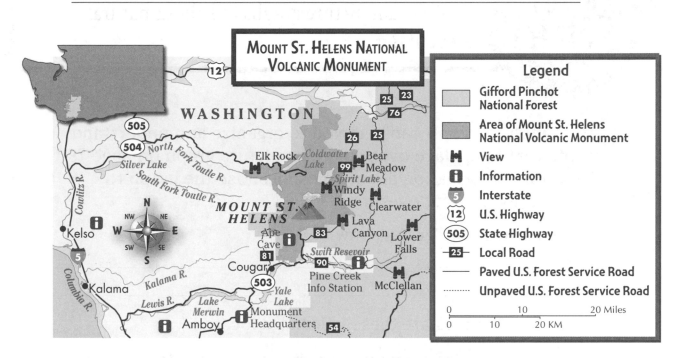

MOUNT ST. HELENS NATIONAL VOLCANIC MONUMENT

Legend

Gifford Pinchot National Forest

Area of Mount St. Helens National Volcanic Monument

ℍ View

ℹ Information

⑤ Interstate

⑫ U.S. Highway

⑤⓪⑤ State Highway

25 Local Road

—— Paved U.S. Forest Service Road

········ Unpaved U.S. Forest Service Road

0   10   20 Miles

0   10   20 KM

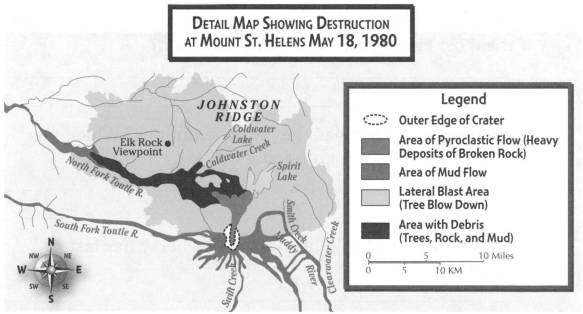

DETAIL MAP SHOWING DESTRUCTION AT MOUNT ST. HELENS MAY 18, 1980

Legend

⟨ ⟩ Outer Edge of Crater

Area of Pyroclastic Flow (Heavy Deposits of Broken Rock)

Area of Mud Flow

Lateral Blast Area (Tree Blow Down)

Area with Debris (Trees, Rock, and Mud)

0   5   10 Miles

0   5   10 KM

SOURCE: Based on information from the U.S. Forest Service and U.S. Geological Survey

Read a Picture Graph

What can picture graphs tell about natural events?

A **picture graph** can help you to organize and understand events that take place over time. The picture graph on page 79 gives some information about volcanoes. Use the graph to answer the following questions.

1. What does the graph show?

   _____

   _____

2. In which states are these volcanoes located?

   _____

3. Of all the volcanoes shown on the map, which one has had the most eruptions? How many has it had?

   _____

   _____

4. Which volcano has had the fewest eruptions? Which has had the most recent eruptions?

   _____

   _____

5. About how long has it been since Newberry has last erupted?

   _____

Learn more about the science and the effects of volcanoes. Refer to the Diagram of a Volcano on Appendix page 105 and the information on pages 76–77. Answer the following question.

6. How do volcanoes cause damage?

_____

_____

_____

_____

7. Now you will do research in the library to learn more about volcanoes. On a separate piece of paper, write at least two short paragraphs about one of the following volcanic eruptions:
- Kilauea (1983)
- Mauna Loa (1984)
- Lassen Peak (1921)
- Katmai (1912)

In your report, tell where the volcano is located and when it erupted, the history of the volcano, and the effect on the people who lived near the eruption.

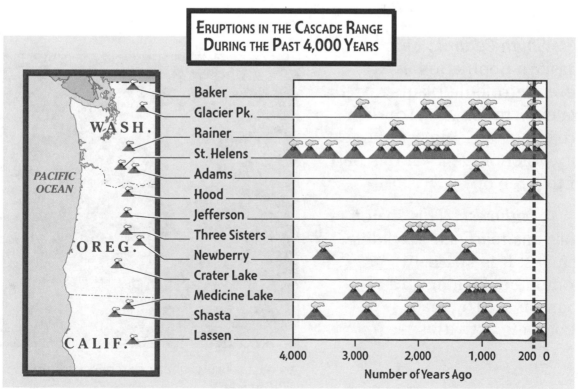

ERUPTIONS IN THE CASCADE RANGE DURING THE PAST 4,000 YEARS

Number of Years Ago

SOURCE: Based on information from the U.S. Geological Survey

Alaska Trails

Alaska is by far the largest state in the United States. Its borders do not connect to any other part of the country. Canada is on Alaska's east. Oceans border Alaska on the south, north, and west.

Alaska is the least densely populated state. It has nearly 34,000 miles of coast. It has more than 3.5 million lakes that are bigger than 20 acres. Glacier ice covers more than 16,000 square miles of land.

Alaska is often divided by geographers into five separate regions:

Inside Passage: Fishing, tourism, and forestry are important to this region. Many small towns, glaciers, and forests are found here. Alaska's state capital, Juneau, is also located here.

South-Central: Most of Alaska's population lives here. Petroleum plants, transportation, and tourism are important. Alaska's largest city, Anchorage, is in this part of this region.

Southwest: This region contains many large wildlife refuges. It is sparsely populated. Fishing and tourism are the main economic activities.

A coastal brown bear catches a salmon in wild Alaska.

Interior: The landscape of this region contains Arctic **tundra** (treeless plains) and large rivers such as the Yukon and Kuskokwim. The state's second-largest city, Fairbanks, is located here. As with the rest of the state, tourism is important.

Far North: Most of this region can be reached only by snowmobile, boat, or airplane. The North Slope and Prudhoe Bay contain large amounts of oil.

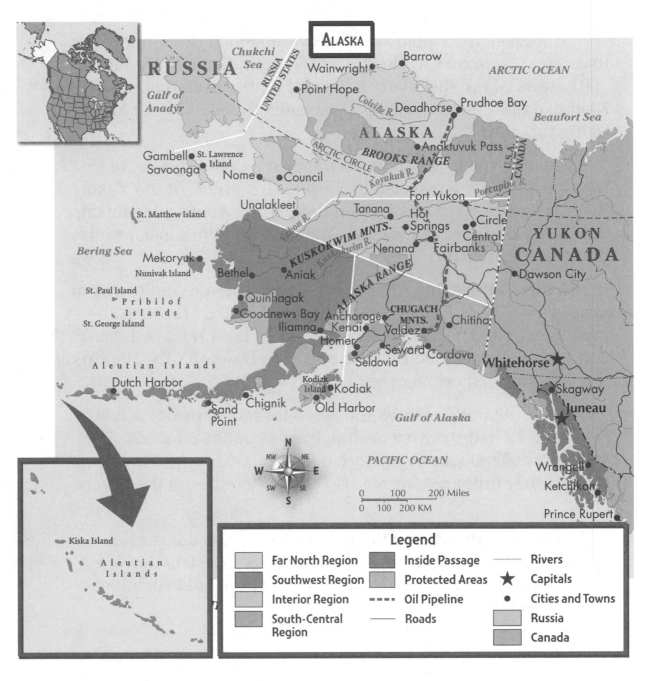

Legend

Far North Region	Inside Passage	— Rivers
Southwest Region	Protected Areas	★ Capitals
Interior Region	- - - Oil Pipeline	• Cities and Towns
South-Central Region	— Roads	Russia
		Canada

Build Your
Map Skills

Read a Map of Adventure

In August 1896, gold was discovered along the Klondike River near Dawson City, in Yukon Territory, Canada. By July 1897, news of the discovery had reached the United States. The Klondike Gold Rush began as thousands traveled to the Yukon to dig for gold.

Some of these **prospectors** traveled an all-water route to Dawson City. They traveled by ship to the mouth of the Yukon River in northwest Alaska. From there, they went by steamship up the Yukon River to Dawson City. This was the easiest route, but it was expensive.

A more affordable route was through the Alaskan towns of Skagway or Dyea. From there, prospectors hiked through the mountains into the Yukon Territory. They built rafts or boats, and then they traveled down the river to Dawson City. Hundreds died in the rapids of the river.

The Chilkoot Pass was too steep for mules or horses, so prospectors had to carry or drag their supplies on sleds. The White Pass Trail was even more dangerous. Many prospectors were poorly prepared for the trip and suffered from the severe cold.

Because the route to the gold fields was so dangerous, Canada decided to build a railroad in 1898. Construction was completed in 1900. Unfortunately, by then the gold rush had largely died out.

Refer to the map and answer the following questions.

1. Which trail leads to Happy Camp? Name the camps you would pass through on the way from Dyea to Happy Camp.

_____

_____

_____

2. About how far is it from Dyea to Chilkoot Pass? From Dyea to Bennett?

_____

_____

3. Which trail is the shortest route to Bennett?

_____

4. Which trail does the railroad line follow?

_____

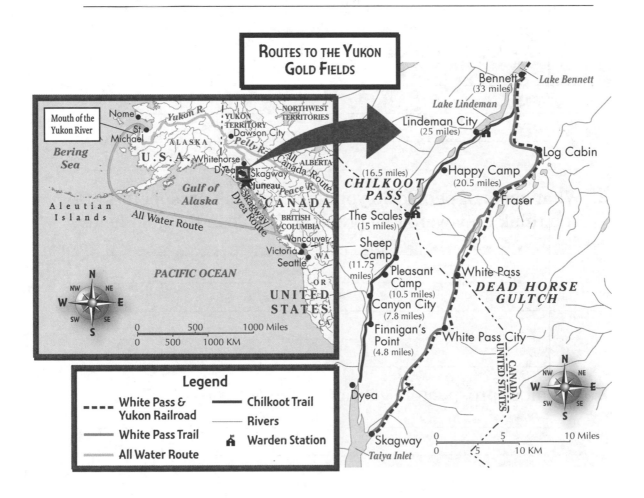

Klondike Adventures

Something to Think About

Why did people leave their homes to risk danger in the wilderness?

Answer these questions about the Klondike Gold Rush and the people who traveled to the Yukon. If necessary, do some library research to help answer the questions.

1. What do you think it was like for the prospectors who crossed the mountains from Skagway and Dyea to the gold fields? What hardships did they face?

_____

_____

_____

_____

2. What kinds of people do you think became prospectors? Do you think they were well-prepared for life in the gold fields?

_____

_____

_____

_____

_____

3. Did most prospectors get rich in the gold fields?

_____

_____

_____

4. What tools did miners use to search for gold?

_____

_____

5. Who else besides prospectors might have made money
from the Klondike Gold Rush?

_____

_____

_____

6. One of the routes shown on the maps on page 83 was
known as a "rich person's route" to the Yukon. Which route
do you think it was? Why?

_____

_____

_____

7. Why do you think that the Chilkoot Trail is a popular
destination for tourists today? Why is this area such an
important part of the cultural history of both Canada and
Alaska?

_____

_____

_____

_____

Merchants sold trade goods to
prospectors at Sheep Camp on the
Chilkoot Trail.

The Hawaiian Islands

In 1959, Hawaii became the 50th state. It is the only state that is completely surrounded by water. Hawaii is a chain of islands that stretches about 1,500 miles across the Pacific Ocean. This state is about 2,300 miles from the **mainland** United States.

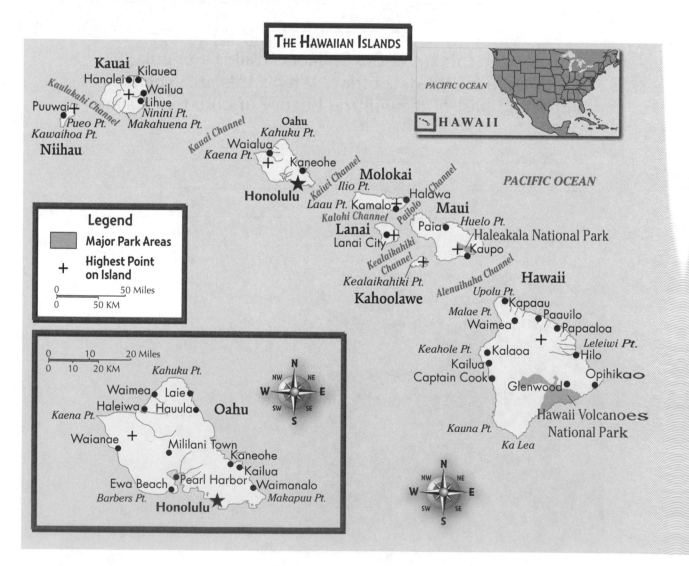

THE HAWAIIAN ISLANDS

Legend
- Major Park Areas
- + Highest Point on Island
- 0   50 Miles
- 0   50 KM

Of the 19 Hawaiian Islands, the eight larger ones at the southeastern end of the island chain are considered the main islands. These islands are Niihau, Kauai, Oahu, Molokai, Lanai, Kahoolawe, Maui, and the island of Hawaii. The capital city, Honolulu, is located on the island of Oahu.

The Hawaiian Islands were formed by volcanoes rising from the floor of the Pacific Ocean. Many volcanoes, especially on the southern part of the island of Hawaii, are still active. Because the islands are so remote, they have many plants and animals that are unique. The climate is milder than most tropical areas, mostly because of the surrounding ocean.

People first arrived on the Hawaiian Islands about 2,000 years ago. They probably came from the Polynesian Islands in the South Pacific. Europeans showed little interest in the islands until the British arrived there in the late 1700s.

Until the 1890s, Hawaii was an independent nation. The islands were annexed by the United States in 1898. After that, Hawaii was considered a **territory** of the United States until it became a state in 1959.

Agriculture is important to Hawaii. Important products include pineapples, coffee, macadamia nuts, sugar cane, and flowers. You can probably guess that tourism is the largest industry in Hawaii. People love visiting the warm beaches and exploring the volcanic areas of the islands.

The great beauty of the Hawaiian Islands draws thousands of tourists each year.

Build Your
Map Skills

Learn about the Attack on Pearl Harbor

In the 1930s, Japan attacked and conquered parts of China and Southeast Asia and many islands in the Pacific Ocean. During this time, Japan began to fear the power of the U.S. Pacific Fleet.

On December 7, 1941, Japan launched a surprise attack on the United States at Pearl Harbor, Hawaii. Almost immediately, the Japanese damaged or sunk several U.S. ships. Ninety minutes after the attack began, it was over.

The Japanese planes were launched from large ships with flat tops called **aircraft carriers.** The main targets at Pearl Harbor were the U.S. aircraft carriers. Fortunately for the United States, the carriers were away during the attack. The Japanese also failed to destroy oil tanks and ship repair facilities at Pearl Harbor. These later became very important to the U.S. war effort.

The attack sunk or damaged 21 U.S. ships. It also damaged or destroyed 323 U.S. airplanes. About 2,400 American servicemen were killed in the attack, along with many civilians. Most of the damaged U.S. ships were later repaired and used in battle against Japan.

Refer to the map, and answer the following questions.

1. From what general direction did the Japanese planes approach the island of Oahu?

_____

2. Which airfields did the Japanese attack on Oahu?

   _____

3. Where were most of the battleships in relation to Ford
   Island?

   _____

4. Name two ships close to the *Arizona*.

   _____

5. What does the map tell you about the way U.S. battleships
   and cruisers are named?

   _____

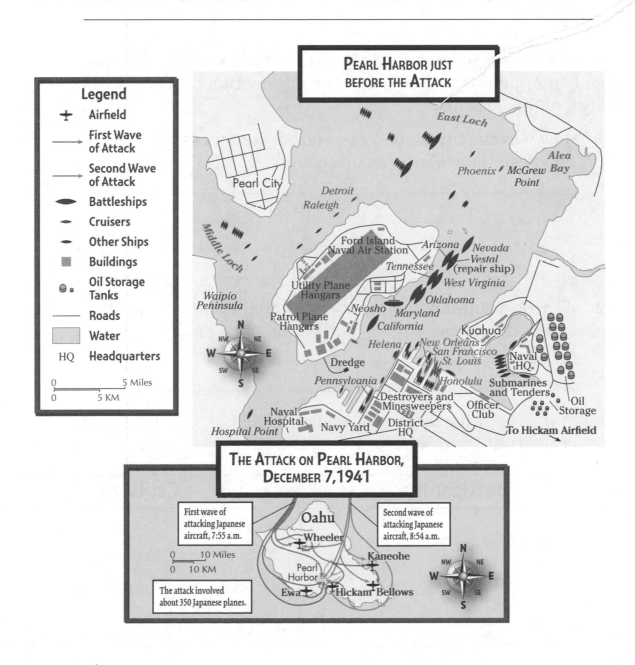

World War II and Pearl Harbor

Something to Think About

What can a war memorial tell about history?

Answer these questions about the attack on Pearl Harbor. Refer to Appendix page 106 and the information on the previous pages of this lesson.

1. How was the attack on Pearl Harbor a success for the Japanese? How was it a failure?

_____

_____

_____

_____

2. Why do you think the Japanese wanted to attack the ships within the harbor rather than on the open sea?

_____

_____

3. In the following table, make a list of the U.S. battleships and cruisers at Pearl Harbor during the attack.

Battleships	Cruisers

4. A **memorial** is something that helps us remember a person or important event. A memorial to the *USS Arizona* sits today in Pearl Harbor. Why do you think special attention is given to the *Arizona?*

_____

_____

_____

_____

_____

Do some research to find a war memorial in or near your community. Answer the following questions. If necessary, use a separate piece of paper for your answers.

5. What people or events does the memorial honor? When did these events take place?

_____

_____

_____

_____

6. What does the memorial tell about the people who fought in battle?

_____

_____

_____

_____

Photo by PH1(AW) William R. Goodwin

This memorial is built over the sunken hull of the *Arizona* at Pearl Harbor.

Appendix

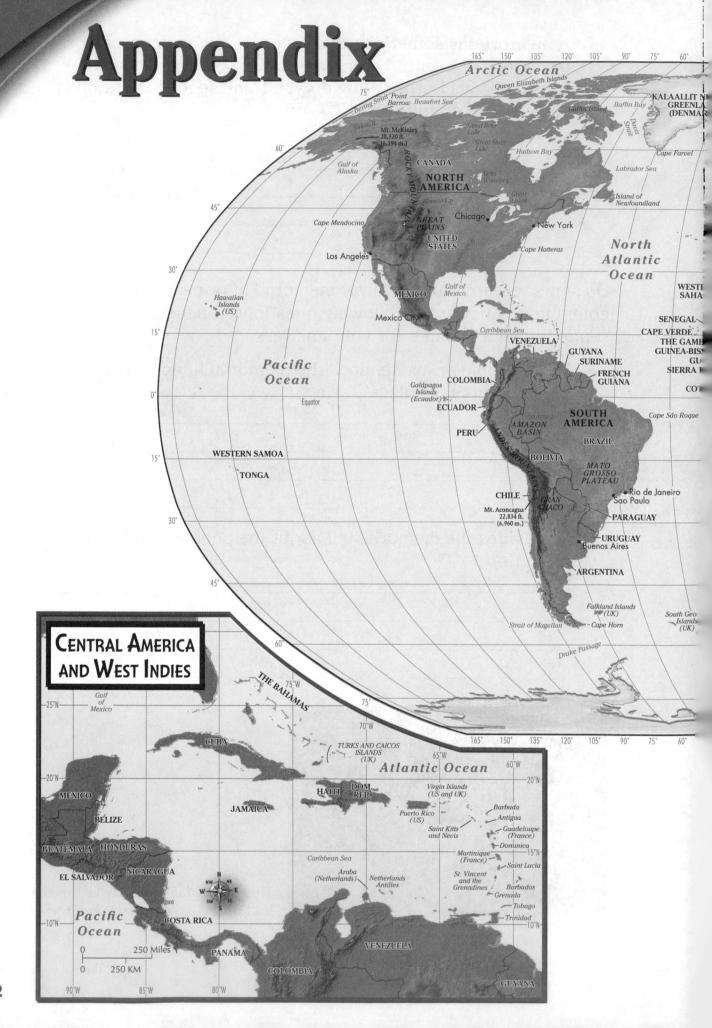

CENTRAL AMERICA AND WEST INDIES

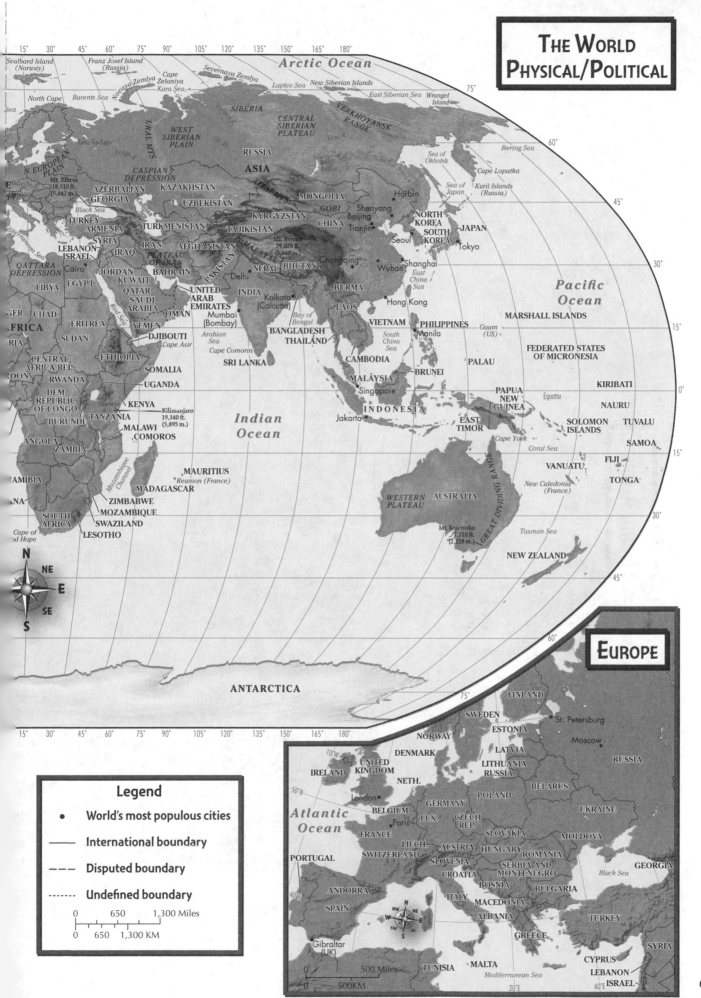

Arctic Ocean

Svalbard Island (Norway)
North Cape
Barents Sea
Franz Josef Island (Russia)
Cape Zelaniya
Novaya Zemlya
Severnaya Zemlya
Kara Sea
Laptev Sea
New Siberian Islands
East Siberian Sea
Wrangel Island
75°

SIBERIA
CENTRAL SIBERIAN PLATEAU
VERKHOYANSK RANGE
Lena R.
Ob R.
Lake Ladoga
N. EUROPEAN PLAIN
URAL MTS.
WEST SIBERIAN PLAIN
Volga R.
RUSSIA
ASIA
Sea of Okhotsk
Cape Lopatka
Bering Sea
60°

Mt. Elbrus 18,510 ft. (5,642 m.)
CASPIAN DEPRESSION
AZERBAIJAN
GEORGIA
Black Sea
Caspian Sea
KAZAKHSTAN
UZBEKISTAN
Aral Sea
ALTAI MTS.
MONGOLIA
GOBI
Harbin
Shenyang
Beijing
Tianjin
NORTH KOREA
SOUTH KOREA
Sea of Japan
Kuril Islands (Russia)
JAPAN
45°

TURKEY
ARMENIA
SYRIA
LEBANON
ISRAEL
IRAQ
IRAN
Mediterranean Sea
TURKMENISTAN
KYRGYZSTAN
TAJIKISTAN
AFGHANISTAN
PLATEAU OF IRAN
HIMALAYAS
Mt. Everest 29,028 ft. (8,848 m.)
CHINA
Chongqing
Seoul
Wuhan
Shanghai
East China Sea
Tokyo
30°

QATTARA DEPRESSION
Cairo
JORDAN
KUWAIT
QATAR
BAHRAIN
SAUDI ARABIA
UNITED ARAB EMIRATES
OMAN
PAKISTAN
NEPAL
Delhi
BHUTAN
INDIA
BURMA
Kolkata (Calcutta)
Hong Kong
Pacific Ocean

LIBYA
EGYPT
Red Sea
YEMEN
Mumbai (Bombay)
Arabian Sea
Cape Asir
Bay of Bengal
Cape Comorin
BANGLADESH
THAILAND
LAOS
VIETNAM
South China Sea
PHILIPPINES
Manila
Guam (US)
MARSHALL ISLANDS
15°

CHAD
ERITREA
DJIBOUTI
SUDAN
AFRICA
CENTRAL AFRICA REP.
ETHIOPIA
SOMALIA
UGANDA
SRI LANKA
CAMBODIA
MALAYSIA
Singapore
BRUNEI
PALAU
FEDERATED STATES OF MICRONESIA
KIRIBATI
0°
Equator

RWANDA
DEM REPUBLIC OF CONGO
BURUNDI
KENYA
TANZANIA
Lake Victoria
Kilimanjaro 19,340 ft. (5,895 m.)
MALAWI
COMOROS
INDONESIA
Jakarta
PAPUA NEW GUINEA
EAST TIMOR
Cape York
SOLOMON ISLANDS
NAURU
TUVALU
SAMOA

ANGOLA
ZAMBIA
Indian Ocean
MAURITIUS
Reunion (France)
Coral Sea
VANUATU
New Caledonia (France)
FIJI
TONGA
15°

NAMIBIA
Mozambique Channel
MADAGASCAR
ZIMBABWE
MOZAMBIQUE
SWAZILAND
LESOTHO
SOUTH AFRICA
Cape of Good Hope
WESTERN PLATEAU
AUSTRALIA
Mt. Kosciusko 7,310 ft. (2,228 m.)
GREAT DIVIDING RANGE
Tasman Sea
NEW ZEALAND
30°

N
NE
E
SE
S

45°

60°

75°

ANTARCTICA

15° 30° 45° 60° 75° 90° 105° 120° 135° 150° 165° 180°

FINLAND
SWEDEN
St. Petersburg
NORWAY
ESTONIA
Moscow
LATVIA
LITHUANIA
RUSSIA
RUSSIA
DENMARK
UNITED KINGDOM
IRELAND
NETH.
London
BELGIUM
LUX.
Paris
FRANCE
GERMANY
POLAND
BELARUS
UKRAINE
Atlantic Ocean
CZECH REP.
SLOVAKIA
MOLDOVA
PORTUGAL
LIECH.
SWITZERLAND
AUSTRIA
HUNGARY
ROMANIA
SLOVENIA
CROATIA
SERBIA AND MONTENEGRO
BOSNIA
GEORGIA
Black Sea
ANDORRA
SPAIN
ITALY
MACEDONIA
BULGARIA
ALBANIA
TURKEY
Gibraltar (UK)
GREECE
SYRIA
TUNISIA
MALTA
Mediterranean Sea
CYPRUS
LEBANON
ISRAEL

10°W
50°N
40°N
20°E
40°E

N
NW NE
W E
SW SE
S

0 500 Miles
0 500KM

Legend

- **World's most populous cities**
- —— **International boundary**
- – – – **Disputed boundary**
- ······ **Undefined boundary**

0 650 1,300 Miles
0 650 1,300 KM

NORTH AMERICA

North Pole

RUSSIA

Bering Sea
Saint Lawrence Island
Bering Strait
Chukchi Sea
Point Barrow
Beaufort Sea

SEWARD PEN.
BROOKS RANGE
Fairbanks
Yukon R.
Mt. McKinley 20,320 ft. (6,194 m.)
ALASKA RANGE
Anchorage
Gulf of Alaska

Arctic Ocean

Banks Island
Victoria Island
Great Bear Lake
Mackenzie R.
MACKENZIE MOUNTAINS
Mt. Logan 19,551 ft. (5,959 m.)
Whitehorse
Juneau
Alexander Archipelago
Queen Charlotte Islands
Vancouver Island
Victoria
Vancouver
COAST MOUNTAINS
ROCKY MOUNTAINS
Fraser R.

Queen Elizabeth Islands
Ellesmere Island
Nares Strait
Prince of Wales Island
BOOTHIA PEN.
Baffin Island
MELVILLE PEN.
Baffin Bay
Davis Strait

KALAALLIT NUNAAT (GREENLAND) (DENMARK)

Greenland Sea
Denmark Strait
ICELAND
Cape Farewell
Labrador Sea

CANADIAN SHIELD
Great Slave Lake
Lake Athabasca
Peace R.
Athabasca R.
North Saskatchewan R.
south
Lake Athabasca
Churchill R.
Churchill
Hudson Bay
Hudson Strait
UNGAVA PEN.
Ungava Bay
LABRADOR
Smallwood Res.
Newfoundland
Cape Houe

Edmonton
Calgary
Lake Winnipeg
Nelson R.
CANADA

60°N
60°N
75°N
75°N
180°W
165°W
150°W
75°W
60°N
0°
15°W

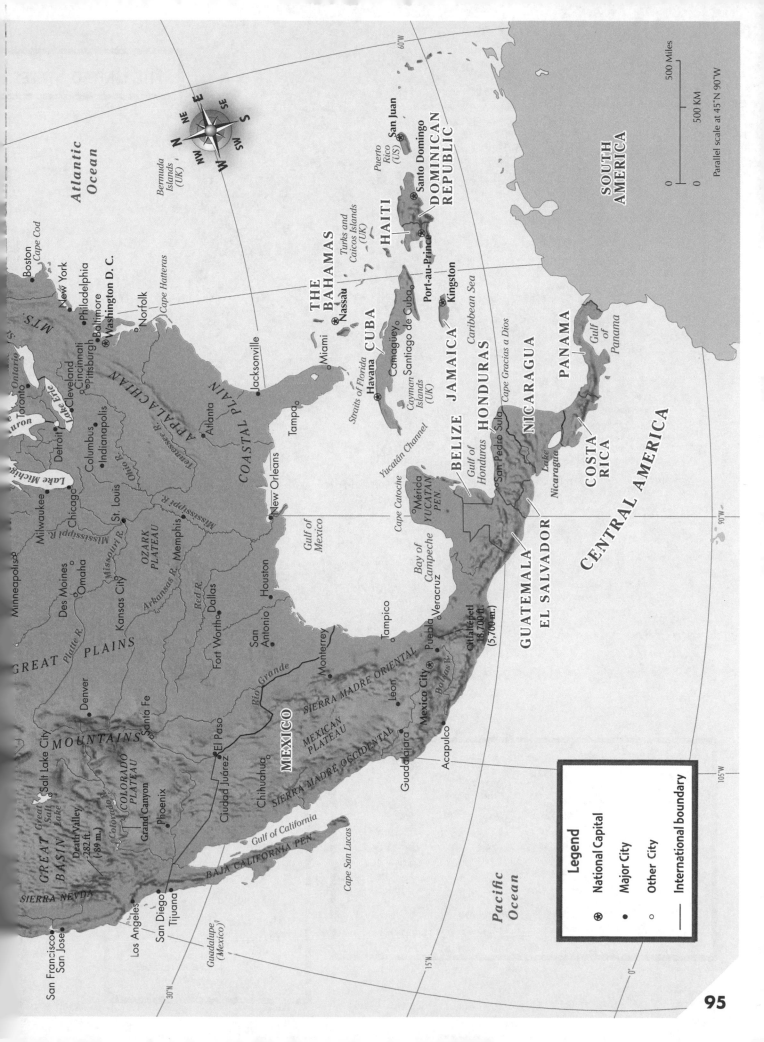

Atlantic Ocean

Bermuda Islands (UK)

Boston
Cape Cod
New York
Philadelphia
Baltimore
Washington D. C.
Cincinnati
Pittsburgh
Cleveland
Norfolk
Cape Hatteras

APPALACHIAN MTS.

Lake Ontario
Lake Erie
Toronto
Detroit
Columbus
Indianapolis
Lake Michigan
Lake Huron
Chicago
Milwaukee
Minneapolis
Des Moines
Omaha
Kansas City

OZARK PLATEAU

St. Louis
Memphis

Tennessee R.
Ohio R.
Missouri R.
Mississippi R.
Arkansas R.
Red R.

GREAT PLAINS

Platte R.

Denver
Santa Fe

MOUNTAINS

COLORADO PLATEAU

Colorado R.

Grand Canyon
Phoenix

GREAT BASIN

Great Salt Lake
Salt Lake City
Death Valley 282 ft. (89 m.)

SIERRA NEVADA

San Francisco
San Jose
Los Angeles
San Diego
Tijuana

Guadalupe (Mexico)

BAJA CALIFORNIA PEN.

Gulf of California

Cape San Lucas

Pacific Ocean

Jacksonville
Atlanta

COASTAL PLAIN

Tampa
New Orleans
Houston
San Antonio
Fort Worth
Dallas
Red R.

Miami
Straits of Florida

Gulf of Mexico

Tampico
Veracruz
Monterrey
León
Mexico City
Balsas R.
Puebla
Acapulco
Guadalajara

MEXICO

SIERRA MADRE ORIENTAL
MEXICAN PLATEAU
SIERRA MADRE OCCIDENTAL

Chihuahua
Ciudad Juárez
El Paso

Rio Grande

Orizaba 18,700 ft. (5,700 m.)

THE BAHAMAS
Nassau

CUBA
Havana
Camagüey
Santiago de Cuba

Cayman Islands (UK)

Yucatán Channel

Cape Catoche
Mérida
YUCATAN PEN.

Bay of Campeche

Gulf of Honduras

BELIZE
GUATEMALA
EL SALVADOR
San Pedro Sula
HONDURAS

Turks and Caicos Islands (UK)

HAITI
Port-au-Prince

JAMAICA
Kingston

Puerto Rico (US)
San Juan

Santo Domingo
DOMINICAN REPUBLIC

Caribbean Sea

Cape Gracias a Dios

NICARAGUA
Lake Nicaragua

COSTA RICA

PANAMA
Gulf of Panama

CENTRAL AMERICA

SOUTH AMERICA

500 Miles
500 KM
Parallel scale at 45°N 90°W
0
0

60°W
90°W
105°W
30°N
15°N
0°

N
NE
NW
E
W
SE
SW
S

Legend

⊛ National Capital
● Major City
○ Other City
— International boundary

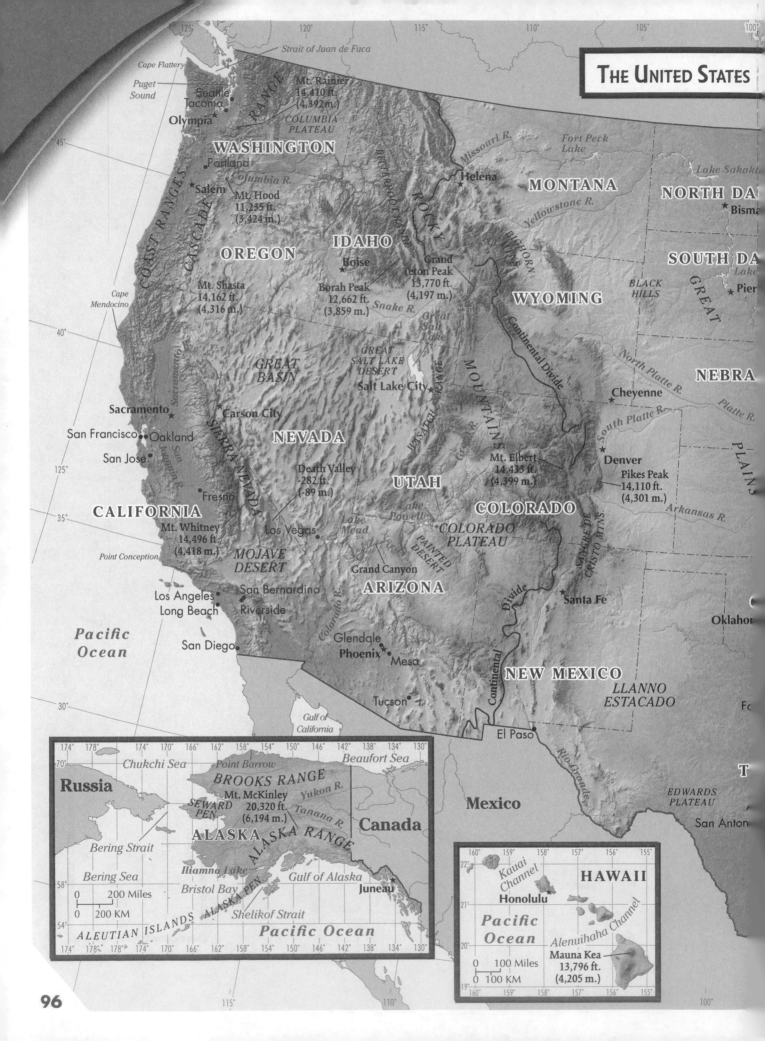

Strait of Juan de Fuca

Cape Flattery

Puget
Sound

Seattle
Tacoma

Olympia

RANGE

Mt. Rainier
14,410 ft.
(4,392m.)

COLUMBIA
PLATEAU

Fort Peck
Lake

Lake Sakaka

WASHINGTON

Portland

Columbia R.

Salem

Mt. Hood
11,235 ft.
(3,424 m.)

CASCADE

COAST RANGES

ROCKY

Missouri R.

Helena

Yellowstone R.

MONTANA

NORTH DA

Bisma

BITTERROOT RANGE

OREGON

IDAHO

Boise

Grand
Teton Peak
13,770 ft.
(4,197 m.)

SOUTH DA

Lake

Cape
Mendocino

Mt. Shasta
14,162 ft.
(4,316 m.)

Borah Peak
12,662 ft.
(3,859 m.)

Snake R.

BIGHORN

WYOMING

BLACK
HILLS

Pier

GREAT

Great
Salt
Lake

Continental Divide

North Platte R.

NEBRA

GREAT
SALT LAKE
DESERT

Sacramento R.

GREAT
BASIN

Salt Lake City

WASATCH RANGE

Cheyenne

South Platte R.

Platte R.

Sacramento

Carson City

San Francisco

Oakland

San Jose

SIERRA NEVADA

San Joaquin R.

NEVADA

Death Valley
-282 ft.
(-89 m.)

Green R.

MOUNTAINS

Mt. Elbert
14,433 ft.
(4,399 m.)

Denver

Pikes Peak
14,110 ft.
(4,301 m.)

PLAINS

Fresno

Las Vegas

Lake
Mead

Lake
Powell

UTAH

COLORADO

Arkansas R.

CALIFORNIA

Mt. Whitney
14,496 ft.
(4,418 m.)

COLORADO
PLATEAU

SANGRE DE CRISTO MTNS.

Point Conception

MOJAVE
DESERT

PAINTED
DESERT

Los Angeles

Long Beach

San Bernardino

Riverside

Grand Canyon

Colorado R.

ARIZONA

Divide

Santa Fe

San Diego

Glendale

Phoenix

Mesa

NEW MEXICO

LLANNO
ESTACADO

Oklahor

Pacific
Ocean

Continental

Tucson

T

Gulf of
California

El Paso

Rio Grande

Fo

Mexico

EDWARDS
PLATEAU

San Anton

ALEUTIAN ISLANDS

ALASKA PEN.

Chukchi Sea

Point Barrow

BROOKS RANGE

Beaufort Sea

Russia

SEWARD
PEN

Mt. McKinley
20,320 ft.
(6,194 m.)

Yukon R.

Tanana R.

Canada

Bering Strait

ALASKA

ALASKA RANGE

Bering Sea

Iliamna Lake

Bristol Bay

Gulf of Alaska

Shelikof Strait

Juneau

0   200 Miles

0   200 KM

Pacific Ocean

Kauai
Channel

HAWAII

Honolulu

Pacific
Ocean

Alenuihaha Channel

Mauna Kea
13,796 ft.
(4,205 m.)

0   100 Miles

0   100 KM

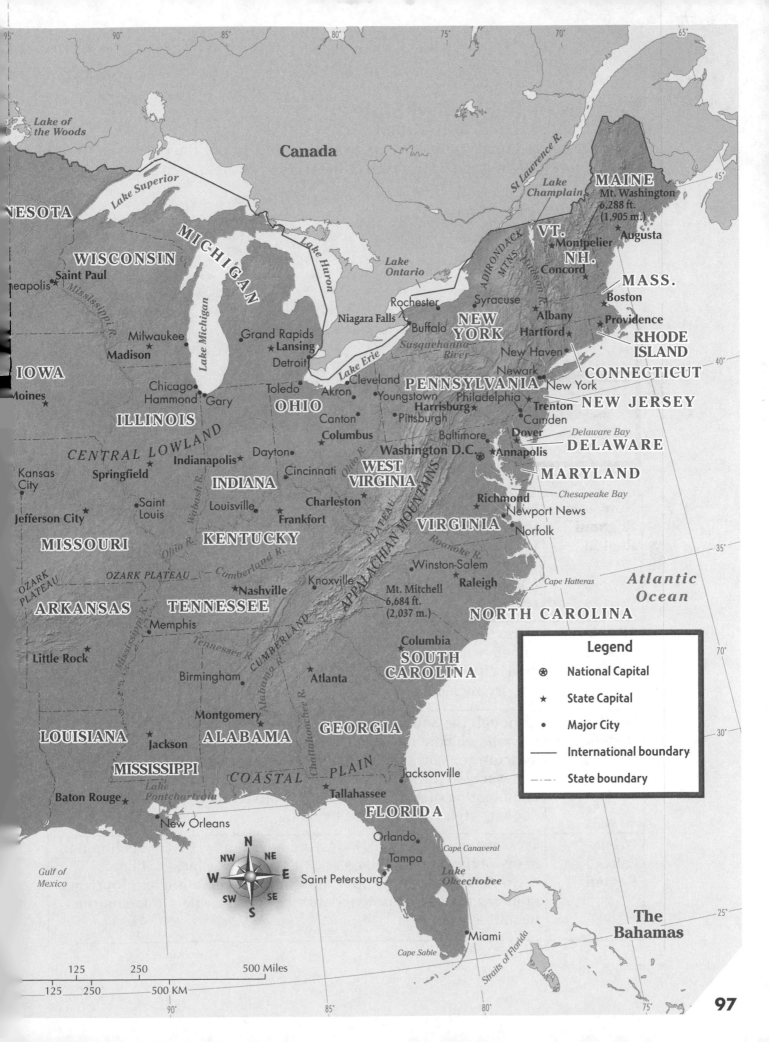

Lake of
the Woods

Canada

Lake Superior

MICHIGAN

Lake Huron

St Lawrence R.

Lake
Champlain

MAINE
Mt. Washington
6,288 ft.
(1,905 m.)

Augusta

VT.
Montpelier

MINNESOTA

WISCONSIN

Saint Paul

Lake
Ontario

ADIRONDACK MTNS.

NH.
Concord

MASS.
Boston

Minneapolis

Mississippi R.

Milwaukee

Lake Michigan

Grand Rapids

Rochester

Syracuse

Hudson R.

Madison

Lansing

Niagara Falls

Buffalo

Albany

Providence

RHODE
ISLAND

IOWA

Detroit

Chicago

Toledo

Lake Erie

Cleveland

NEW
YORK

Hartford

New Haven

CONNECTICUT

Susquehanna
River

Des Moines

Hammond

Gary

OHIO

Akron

Youngstown

Newark

New York

NEW JERSEY

ILLINOIS

Canton

Harrisburg

PENNSYLVANIA

Philadelphia

Trenton

Pittsburgh

Camden

CENTRAL LOWLAND

Columbus

Baltimore

Dover

Delaware Bay

DELAWARE

Kansas
City

Springfield

Indianapolis

Dayton

Washington D.C.

Annapolis

MARYLAND

Jefferson City

Saint
Louis

INDIANA

Cincinnati

WEST
VIRGINIA

Ohio R.

Chesapeake Bay

Louisville

Frankfort

Charleston

Richmond

Newport News

VIRGINIA

Wabash R.

MISSOURI

KENTUCKY

Ohio R.

PLATEAU

APPALACHIAN MOUNTAINS

Norfolk

OZARK PLATEAU

Cumberland R.

Roanoke R.

35°

OZARK
PLATEAU

Nashville

Knoxville

Winston-Salem

Cape Hatteras

Atlantic
Ocean

ARKANSAS

TENNESSEE

Mt. Mitchell
6,684 ft.
(2,037 m.)

Raleigh

Memphis

Tennessee R.

CUMBERLAND

NORTH CAROLINA

Little Rock

Mississippi R.

Columbia

Alabama R.

Birmingham

SOUTH
CAROLINA

Atlanta

70°

Legend

⊛ National Capital

★ State Capital

• Major City

—— International boundary

–·–·– State boundary

LOUISIANA

Jackson

ALABAMA

Montgomery

GEORGIA

Chattahoochee R.

30°

MISSISSIPPI

COASTAL PLAIN

Jacksonville

Baton Rouge

Lake
Pontchartrain

Tallahassee

FLORIDA

New Orleans

N

Orlando

Cape Canaveral

Gulf of
Mexico

NW NE

W E

SW SE

S

Tampa

Saint Petersburg

Lake
Okeechobee

25°

The
Bahamas

Miami

Cape Sable

Straits of Florida

125 250 500 Miles

125 250 500 KM

97

Regions of the United States

Note: These are broad statements, or *generalizations,* about the regions of the United States. See Lesson 2 for a map of the regions of the United States.

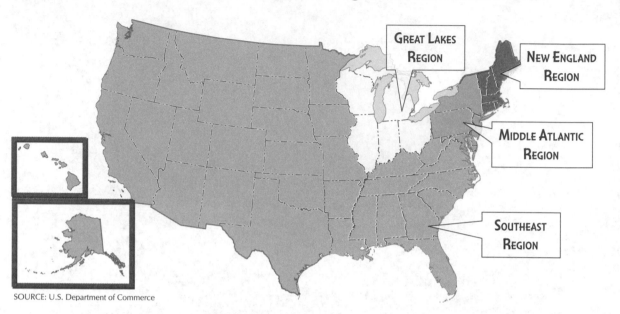

SOURCE: U.S. Department of Commerce

New England Region	New England is the smallest U.S. region. Traditional industries there have included shipbuilding, fishing, trade, and manufacturing. The region is home to many of America's best universities, such as Harvard and Yale. The historic wood houses and numerous lighthouses along the Atlantic coast define the region.
Middle Atlantic Region	This region has some of the country's largest cities and is an area of heavy industry, including steel manufacturing. Many of the great cities of the region, such as New York, New York, are important seaports.
Southeast Region	Although the Southeast has become a key manufacturing region, the mild climate has always encouraged a wide variety of agriculture. Many styles of music (notably jazz and country) are associated with the region. The area's distinctive food—a combination of African American, Native American, and European cooking styles—is enjoyed by many.
Great Lakes Region	This region is America's industrial heartland. The area is home to many of the country's largest cities, such as Chicago, Illinois. The region also boasts an important outdoor recreation and tourism industry that welcomes visitors who want to spend time on the beautiful lakes.

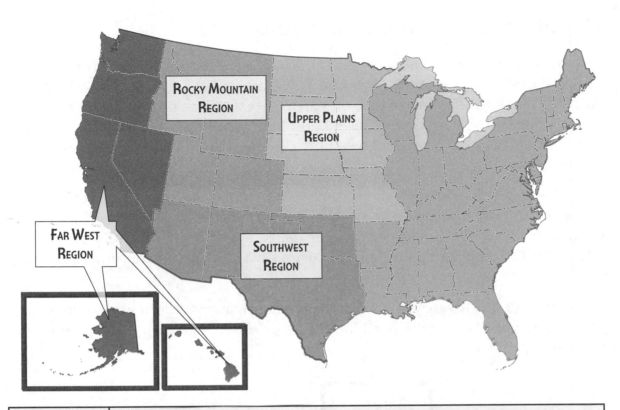

Upper Plains Region	The fertile soil of the Upper Plains Region produces abundant harvests of grains such as wheat and oats. Many European immigrants from Germany, Sweden, and Norway originally settled on the Plains, bringing their culture with them.
Rocky Mountain Region	Most of the Rocky Mountain region is sparsely populated and mountainous. Much of the area is quite dry. Common economic activities there include ranching, lumbering, and mining.
Southwest Region	This region contrasts with the adjacent Upper Plains Region in weather (it is drier), population (it is more densely populated), and ethnicity (there are major Hispanic and Native American communities). Outside the cities, wide-open spaces—much of which is desert—dominate the region.
Far West Region	This region is truly an area of contrasts, from the frigid lands of Alaska to the tropical islands of Hawaii. The long growing seasons have made Southern California one of the most important agricultural regions in the world. Yet high-tech computer industries are also key parts of the area's economy. Computer giants such as Microsoft, Intel, and Apple are all located here. Major film and entertainment studios are located here also.

Understanding Latitude and Longitude

The **equator** is an imaginary line drawn around the center of Earth. More lines are drawn parallel to the equator. These are called lines (or parallels) of latitude. The **latitude** of any place on Earth is its distance north or south of the equator, measured in degrees. The equator is 0°. The latitude of the North Pole is 90°N (this is read as "ninety degrees north"). The latitude of the South Pole is 90°S ("ninety degrees south").

The **prime meridian** is an imaginary line around Earth from the North Pole to the South Pole that runs through the city of Greenwich, England. Other lines drawn parallel to the prime meridian are called lines (or meridians) of longitude. Like latitude, **longitude** is measured in degrees. The longitude of New York City is 74°W ("seventy-four degrees west").

The equator divides Earth into the northern and southern hemispheres. The prime meridian divides Earth into the western and eastern hemispheres. **Hemisphere** means *half of a globe*.

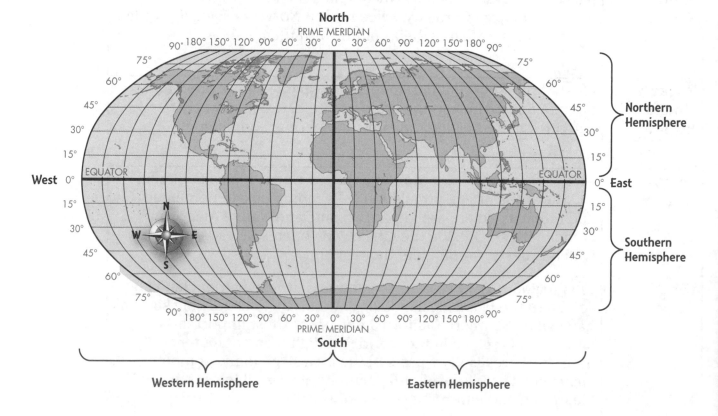

LINES OF LATITUDE AND LONGITUDE

Excerpts from The Declaration of Independence

In Congress, July 4, 1776. The unanimous Declaration of the thirteen united States of America,

The Preamble explains that the 13 states are declaring separation (independence) from Great Britain.

When in the Course of human events, it becomes necessary for one people to dissolve the political bands which have connected them with another [. . .] a decent respect to the opinions of mankind requires that they should declare the causes which impel them to the separation.

The Declaration of Natural Rights explains that people have certain natural rights (called "inalienable rights"). Governments exist through the consent of the people and should protect the rights of the people. If the government fails to do this, then the people have a right to rebel against the government and set up a better government.

We hold these truths to be self-evident, that all men are created equal, that they are endowed by their Creator with certain unalienable Rights, that among these are Life, Liberty and the pursuit of Happiness.

That to secure these rights, Governments are instituted among Men, deriving their just powers from the consent of the governed,

That whenever any Form of Government becomes destructive of these ends, it is the Right of the People to alter or to abolish it, and to institute new Government [. . . .]

This section is a long list of grievances (problems) the 13 states had with Great Britain. (Only a few of them are listed here.) The list explains that King George III has established a "Tyranny" (absolute rule) over the 13 states.

Such has been the patient sufferance of these Colonies; and such is now the necessity which constrains them to alter their former Systems of Government. The history of the present King of Great Britain [George III] is a history of repeated injuries and usurpations, all having in direct object the establishment of an absolute Tyranny over these States. To prove this, let Facts be submitted to a candid world [. . . .]

He has kept among us, in times of peace, Standing Armies without the Consent of our legislature.

He has combined with others to subject us to a jurisdiction foreign to our constitution, and unacknowledged by our laws; giving his Assent to their acts of pretended legislation:

For cutting off our Trade with all parts of the world:

For imposing Taxes on us without our Consent [without political representation]:

For depriving us, in many cases, of the benefits of Trial by Jury: [. . . .]

Lake Superior
Lake Huron
Lake Ontario
Lake Michigan
Lake Erie

Fun Facts about the Great Lakes

Lake Superior

- This is the largest of the Great Lakes. It could hold all of the water in the other four Great Lakes, along with three more Lake Eries!

- Lake Superior is 600 feet above sea level. It is the highest of the Great Lakes.

- Lake Superior is the deepest Great Lake, too. It is as deep as 1,332 feet.

- Because Lake Superior is so deep, it's the coldest of the Great Lakes.

Lake Michigan

- Lake Michigan is the only Great Lake entirely within the United States. Each of the other Great Lakes is partly bordered by Canada.

- Lake Michigan is the second-largest of the Great Lakes in amount of water.

- Lake Michigan's shoreline has some of the world's largest freshwater sand dunes.

- Lake Michigan's greatest depth is 925 feet.

Lake Erie

- Lake Erie is the smallest of the Great Lakes in amount of water.

- Lake Erie's water levels change all the time. It gets water from lakes Superior, Huron, and Michigan.

- Lake Erie is the shallowest Great Lake. Its greatest depth is only about 210 feet.

- Lake Erie is the warmest of the Great Lakes.

Lake Ontario

- Lake Ontario is the smallest of the Great Lakes in area.

- Lake Ontario is the lowest of the Great Lakes. It is only about 243 feet above sea level.

- Boats could not pass from Lake Ontario into the other Great Lakes until locks were built to adjust the water level.

- Lake Ontario is connected to Lake Erie by the Niagara River. Niagara Falls is located where the two lakes meet.

Lake Huron

- Lake Huron has the longest shoreline of any of the Great Lakes.

- Lake Huron is the third-largest Great Lake in amount of water. It is the second-largest Great Lake in area.

- Lake Huron's greatest depth is 750 feet.

Protecting Your Home

 **Floods**

- Think about what you are storing in your basement. It is not a good idea to put irreplaceable items in the basement if you live in an area that may flood. Also, consider that certain items, such as books and clothing, are more likely to be damaged by dampness and mold.

- A flood can damage your utilities. Consider raising your main breaker or fuse box and your utility meters above the level at which your area is likely to flood.

- If you live in an area that is prone to flooding, your family may want to consider buying flood insurance.

 Hurricanes and Tornadoes

- Use storm shutters or plywood to protect windows and glass when severe weather is coming. This may protect you against flying debris like limbs or other objects carried by strong winds.

- If you live in an area where your house may be damaged by high winds, consider having special straps installed to keep the roof attached to the house.

 Earthquakes

- If you live in an area where an earthquake is possible, think about bolting your cabinets to the walls. Put heavy things on the lower shelves. This will help prevent them from falling on you.

- A gas water heater could fall over during an earthquake and break the gas line, so think about attaching it to a wall.

- Talk to an architect or contractor about possibly bolting your house frame to the foundation.

 Wildfires

- If you live in a dry area that is prone to brush fires, create a safety zone around the house. This would be a clear area separating your home from plants and bushes that can burn easily. Dead brush and grass should be cleared away from your property.

- Put tile or flame-retardant shingles on your roof instead of wood shakes or standard shingles. This will cut the chance that burning debris in the air will catch your roof on fire.

Native Americans Today

Ten Largest Native American Tribes	
Name	**Population**
Cherokee	729,533
Navajo	298,197
Latin American Indian	180,940
Choctaw	158,774
Sioux	153,360
Chippewa	149,669
Apache	96,833
Blackfeet	85,750
Iroquois	80,822
Pueblo	74,085

Selected Native American Reservations in the United States		
Name	**Location**	**Population**
Navajo Nation	Arizona, New Mexico, Utah	175,228
Cherokee	Oklahoma	104,482
Creek	Oklahoma	77,253
Lumbee	North Carolina	62,327
Choctaw	Oklahoma	39,984
Cook Inlet	Alaska	35,972
Chickasaw	Oklahoma	32,372
Calista	Alaska	20,353
United Houma Nation	Louisiana	15,305
Sealaska	Alaska	15,059
Pine Ridge	South Dakota, Nebraska	14,484
Doyon	Alaska	14,128
Kiowa, Comanche, Apache, Fort Sill Apache	Oklahoma	13,045
Fort Apache	Arizona	11,854
Citizen Band Potawatomi Nation–Absentee Shawnee	Oklahoma	10,617
Gila River	Arizona	10,578
Cheyenne/Arapaho	Oklahoma	10,310
Tohono O'odham	Arizona	9,794
Osage	Oklahoma	9,209
Rosebud	South Dakota	9,165
San Carlos	Arizona	9,065
Blackfeet	Montana	8,684

Source: U.S. Geological Survey

Glossary

abolition movement: a political movement that began in the early 1800s to abolish slavery in the United States and its territories

aircraft carrier: a type of large ship with a flat top from which planes can be launched

altitude: the height of the land or an object

annex: to take over or acquire an area of land

basin: an area of lower elevation that drains the surrounding land

bay: a large inlet in a coastline that is set off from a larger water body by points of land

bayou: a small, slow-moving stream from a lake or river that is common in some Southern states

canal: a human-made waterway

cardinal directions: the four main directions (north, south, east, and west)

cartographer: a person who makes maps and globes

channel: a narrow body of water between two points of land

chronological order: arrangement of events, as in a time line, in the order in which they happen

civil war: war between groups of people who belong to the same country, such as the U.S. Civil War (1861–1865)

climate: the typical weather of a specific place on Earth

compass rose: a map symbol that shows directions

conquistador: Spanish soldiers and explorers who conquered much of North and South America for Spain between the 15th and 17th centuries

continent: a large land mass

Continental Divide: a line along the Rocky Mountains to the east of which rivers flow into the Atlantic Ocean or Hudson Bay and to the west of which water flows into the Pacific Ocean

cove: a small inlet in a coastline that is smaller than a bay

cultural history: events in a community or nation that unite the people living there

dam: a barrier people build across a river to control the flow of water

desert: a large, dry region

disaster: an event that causes great suffering and destruction

diversity: variety

ecology: the relationship among plants, animals, and their surroundings

economy: a system of making and transporting products and services

ecosystem: a group of animals and plants living together within an environment

elevation: the height of the land

endangered: plants or animals that are threatened or in danger of dying out

equator: an imaginary line drawn around the center of Earth

erosion: the wearing away of land and soil by wind or the flow of water

expedition: a long, organized journey often through an unexplored area

flood: the overflowing of a body of water onto dry land

flood stage: the point at which a creek or river overflows its banks

globe: a representation of Earth in miniature that imitates its round shape

H

headwaters: the place where a river system begins

hemisphere: half of a globe

hurricane: a large, violent tropical storm

I

imports: products brought into a country from other countries

intermediate directions: directions that are between the cardinal directions (northeast, southeast, northwest, and southwest)

island: land that is surrounded by water on all sides

L

lahar: a mix of rocks, gasses, and water that flows down the slopes of a volcano

lake: a body of water completely surrounded by land that is larger than a pond

landform: the shape or form of a physical feature of Earth's surface, such as a plain, hill, or mountain

latitude: lines on a map or globe drawn east to west, parallel to the equator

lava: very hot, molten rock that flows from a volcano

legend: a box on a map that explains what each symbol on the map means

levee: a barrier people build to hold back the flow of water

longitude: lines on a map or globe drawn from north to south, parallel to the prime meridian

lock: small area of a waterway where the water level can be raised or lowered to allow passage

M

magma: rock below Earth's surface that is made liquid by high pressure and temperature

mainland: the main land area of a country

map: a flat representation of Earth

memorial: something that helps us remember a person or important event

mesa: a high area of land with a flat top and sides that are usually steep cliffs; smaller than a plateau

navigable waterway: a waterway that can be traveled on by a ship

North Pole: the most northern point on Earth

ocean: the large body of salt water that covers most of the surface of Earth

peninsula: land with water on three sides that extends into a body of water such as a lake or ocean

physical map: a map that shows a region's landforms and water forms

picture graph: a graph that presents data using icons or symbols

plantation: a large farm common in the American South before the Civil War

plateau: a high area of flat land

political boundaries: human-made, invisible boundaries, such as state borders

population density: a measure of the number of people who live per square mile in an area

precipitation: liquid or solid water that falls from the atmosphere to Earth

prime meridian: an imaginary line around Earth from top to bottom that runs through the city of Greenwich, England

prospector: someone who explores an area for minerals such as gold or silver

pueblo: a kind of living area made from stone or mud bricks

pyroclastic flow: a combination of hot, dry pieces of rock and hot gases that are discharged from a volcano at high speeds

region: an area that has certain characteristics that make it different from other areas

reservation: an area established by the U.S. government for Native American use

river: a large, natural stream of water that is larger than a creek

Answer Key

Page 5:

Latitude: At the equator, the sun's rays hit at a direct angle. This makes the air temperature very hot. As you move toward the poles, the Sun's rays become cooler due to the curved surface of Earth.

Altitude: It is usually cool on top of a mountain even in summer. This is because a mountaintop is at a high **altitude.**

Winds: Winds from hot areas of Earth raise temperatures and those from cold areas lower temperatures. Winds influence the amount of **precipitation** (rain or snow) each area gets.

Distance from the sea: Land near the sea has more moderate seasons than areas that are inland.

The climate map shows six different climate zones. Notice that there are numbers on the map in different climate zones. In the table, write the name of the continent where the number is located. Then, write a description of the climate.

	Continent	Description of the Climate
1	Africa	Tropical (hot and wet all year)
2	Australia	Arid (dry and hot all year)
3	Europe	Temperate (cold winters and mild summers)
4	Africa	Arid (dry and hot all year)
5	Asia	Mountains (cold all year)
6	Europe	Mediterranean (mild winters and dry, hot summers)
7	Asia	Polar (very cold and dry all year)
8	North America	Temperate (cold winters and mild summers)
9	South America	Tropical (hot and wet all year)

5

Page 6:

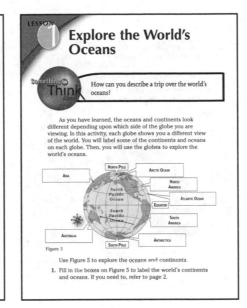

LESSON 1

Explore the World's Oceans

Something to Think About

How can you describe a trip over the world's oceans?

As you have learned, the oceans and continents look different depending upon which side of the globe you are viewing. In this activity, each globe shows you a different view of the world. You will label some of the continents and oceans on each globe. Then, you will use the globes to explore the world's oceans.

Figure 5

Use Figure 5 to explore the oceans and continents.

1. Fill in the boxes on Figure 5 to label the world's continents and oceans. If you need to, refer to page 2.

6

Page 7:

2. Plan your trip. Start at the southern tip of South America. From there, draw a line to eastern Australia. The line you draw shows the way you will travel. Answer these questions to describe your trip.

What continent will you pass to the south? **Antarctica**

What ocean will you cross? **the Pacific**

What direction will you travel? **west or northwest**

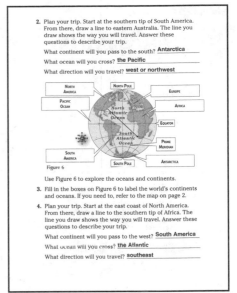

Figure 6

Use Figure 6 to explore the oceans and continents.

3. Fill in the boxes on Figure 6 to label the world's continents and oceans. If you need to, refer to the map on page 2.

4. Plan your trip. Start at the east coast of North America. From there, draw a line to the southern tip of Africa. The line you draw shows the way you will travel. Answer these questions to describe your trip.

What continent will you pass to the west? **South America**

What ocean will you cross? **the Atlantic**

What direction will you travel? **southeast**

7

Page 11:

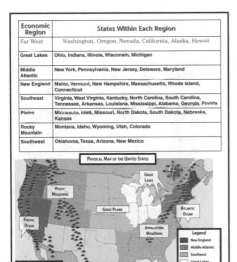

Economic Region	States Within Each Region
Far West	Washington, Oregon, Nevada, California, Alaska, Hawaii
Great Lakes	Ohio, Indiana, Illinois, Wisconsin, Michigan
Middle Atlantic	New York, Pennsylvania, New Jersey, Delaware, Maryland
New England	Maine, Vermont, New Hampshire, Massachusetts, Rhode Island, Connecticut
Southeast	Virginia, West Virginia, Kentucky, North Carolina, South Carolina, Tennessee, Arkansas, Louisiana, Mississippi, Alabama, Georgia, Florida
Plains	Minnesota, Iowa, Missouri, North Dakota, South Dakota, Nebraska, Kansas
Rocky Mountain	Montana, Idaho, Wyoming, Utah, Colorado
Southwest	Oklahoma, Texas, Arizona, New Mexico

11

Page 12:

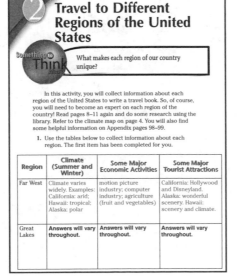

LESSON 2

Travel to Different Regions of the United States

Something to Think About

What makes each region of our country unique?

In this activity, you will collect information about each region of the United States to write a travel book. So, of course, you will need to become an expert on each region of the country! Read pages 8–11 again and do some research using the library. Refer to the climate map on page 4. You will also find some helpful information on Appendix pages 98–99.

1. Use the tables below to collect information about each region. The first item has been completed for you.

Region	Climate (Summer and Winter)	Some Major Economic Activities	Some Major Tourist Attractions
Far West	Climate varies widely. Examples: California: arid; Hawaii: tropical; Alaska: polar	motion picture industry; computer industry; agriculture (fruit and vegetables)	California: Hollywood and Disneyland. Alaska: wonderful scenery. Hawaii: scenery and climate.
Great Lakes	Answers will vary throughout.	Answers will vary throughout.	Answers will vary throughout.

12

Page 13:

Region	Climate (Summer and Winter)	Some Major Economic Activities	Some Major Tourist Attractions
Middle Atlantic			
New England			
Southeast			

2. After you have collected all your information, select two regions from the table and write their names below. On a separate piece of paper, write a paragraph for your book describing how the two regions are different. **Answers will vary.**

3. Now, select one of the regions and create a travel poster that reflects that region's characteristics. You will use the poster to help sell your book in bookstores located throughout that region. On a separate piece of paper, organize the pictures and text that will go on your poster. **Answers will vary.**

13

Answer Key

Page 16

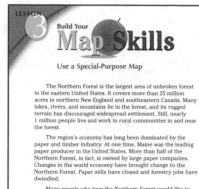

LESSON 3

Build Your Map Skills

Use a Special-Purpose Map

The Northern Forest is the largest area of unbroken forest in the eastern United States. It covers more than 25 million acres in northern New England and southeastern Canada. Many lakes, rivers, and mountains lie in the forest, and its rugged terrain has discouraged widespread settlement. Still, nearly 1 million people live and work in rural communities in and near the forest.

The region's economy has long been dominated by the paper and timber industry. At one time, Maine was the leading paper producer in the United States. More than half of the Northern Forest, in fact, is owned by large paper companies. Changes in the world economy have brought change to the Northern Forest. Paper mills have closed and forestry jobs have dwindled.

Many people who love the Northern Forest would like to work with the paper companies to preserve jobs while also preserving the forest. They see tourism and recreation as a possible source of jobs and income for the region.

In this lesson, you will use the map scale to measure distance. Transfer the scale to a piece of paper and use it to measure the distance.

1. The Northern Forest is in which states on the map?
   New York, Vermont, New Hampshire, and Maine

2. Which state has the greatest part of the Northern Forest?
   Maine

16

Page 17

3. Use the map scale to measure the length of the Northern Forest from Lake Ontario to the northeast tip of Maine. About how long is it? About how wide is it at its widest point in the state of Maine?
   It is about 500 miles long and about 200 miles wide.

4. Name one lake and one river that are located within the Northern Forest. In which states are these lakes?
   Possible answers: Moosehead Lake, Maine; Connecticut River, Vermont/New Hampshire

5. Which state capital is located within the Northern Forest?
   Montpelier, Vermont

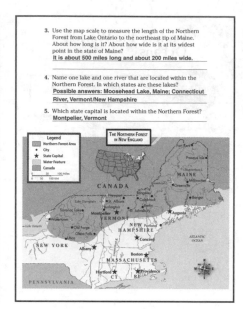

17

Page 18

LESSON 3

Learn about New England

Something to Think About — What natural areas near your home are important to you?

Answer the following questions about New England. Reread the material in this lesson, if necessary.

1. Describe some water forms and landforms that are typical of the Northern Forest region.
   Possible answer: The Northern Forest region has mountains and many lakes and rivers.

2. Why do you think the largest cities in New England are located on the coast?
   This is probably because they are ports that benefit from the ocean as a way to transport goods.

3. What kind of economic problems have developed in the Northern Forest region in recent years? **Many of the paper mills closed, putting people out of work.**

4. What connections do people in the coastal cities like Boston have to the Northern Forest? Why should they care about the economy, resources, and people of that area?
   Possible answer: Products produced from timber in the Northern Forest can be shipped through large port towns like Boston, benefiting the economies of both areas. Many people in large cities use the Northern Forest for recreation.

18

Page 19

5. Select three New England communities. Each community should be from a different state. Do library research to complete the following table.

Name and State of Community	Population	Main Economic Activities	Nearby Attractions
Montpelier, Vermont	8,035	Vermont state government services; finance, insurance, and real estate	Vermont Statehouse; Vermont Historical Society Museum; Vermont Mountaineers baseball
		Answers will vary.	

6. Identify a natural area in your region of the country. Describe it in the space below. As you write, think about these questions: What are the area's attractions? Is it used for recreation or industry? Has there been any change in the way people use the area? Who benefits most from it?
   Answers will vary.

19

Page 22

LESSON 4

Build Your Map Skills

Read a Watershed Map

The map shows the Connecticut River watershed with tributaries and dams. A **tributary** is a smaller stream that flows into a larger river.

Use the map to answer the following questions.

1. What tributaries enter the river at Wilder Dam?
   the Mascoma and White rivers

2. Which dams are shown on tributaries?
   Leesville Dam, Rainbow Dam, DSI Dam, and Townshend Dam

3. In which general direction does the Connecticut River flow?
   south

4. Based on the map scale, about how long is the Connecticut River? Into what body of water does the Connecticut River flow?
   The river is about 300 miles long. It flows into Long Island Sound.

5. The Connecticut River forms the border between what two states?
   Vermont and New Hampshire

22

Page 23

6. Name all of the dams shown on the map in the state of Massachusetts.
   DSI Dam, Holyoke Dam, and Turners Falls Dam

7. What tributaries enter the Connecticut River within the state of Connecticut?
   the Eightmile, Salmon, and Farmington rivers

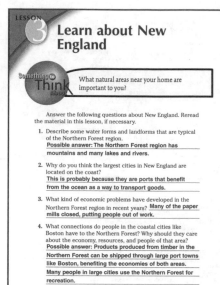

23

Answer Key

LESSON 4 · Restore the River

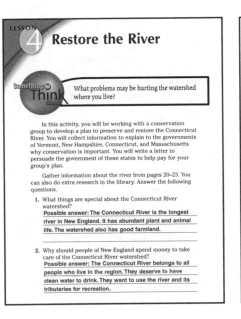

Something to Think About

What problems may be hurting the watershed where you live?

In this activity, you will be working with a conservation group to develop a plan to preserve and restore the Connecticut River. You will collect information to explain to the governments of Vermont, New Hampshire, Connecticut, and Massachusetts why conservation is important. You will write a letter to persuade the government of these states to help pay for your group's plan.

Gather information about the river from pages 20–23. You can also do extra research in the library. Answer the following questions.

1. What things are special about the Connecticut River watershed?
   Possible answer: The Connecticut River is the longest river in New England. It has abundant plant and animal life. The watershed also has good farmland.

2. Why should people of New England spend money to take care of the Connecticut River watershed?
   Possible answer: The Connecticut River belongs to all people who live in the region. They deserve to have clean water to drink. They want to use the river and its tributaries for recreation.

24

---

3. How is the Connecticut River watershed endangered by pollution?
   Possible answer: Pollution comes from many sources, such as fertilizer runoff from farms and lawns or wastewater from houses. It needs to be controlled because it can spoil drinking water.

4. What role do dams play on the river? How do they affect the fish?
   Possible answer: Dams keep certain fish from traveling up the river to spawn. Dams also raise the water temperature, hurting fish populations. Dams also sometimes limit boating and other recreation.

5. How can people benefit from projects that help the Connecticut River?
   Possible answer: Preserving the wetlands can help control flooding downstream that could damage homes. Pollution should be controlled because all people need clean water to drink. Clean water encourages recreation and is good for the economies near the river.

6. All the dams on the river probably cannot be torn down. What else can be done to help the salmon today came from the river to spawn?
   Fish ladders can help the fish get around those dams that must remain in place.

7. Now, write your letter to the governors on a separate piece of paper. Be sure to use the facts you have gathered to convince the governors that it is important to restore and preserve the Connecticut River.
   Answers will vary.

25

LESSON 5 · Build Your Map Skills

Read a Historical Map

The Battle of Long Island was an early battle of the Revolutionary War. American forces under George Washington set up defensive positions around New York City. A large British force massed to the south on Long Island near Flatlands. From there, the British moved their troops so they would be in a position to attack.

While British troops held positions to the south and west of the American positions, another British force advanced on the Americans from the east through Jamaica Pass. This force wanted to get behind the Americans and cut them off from retreat. The British attacked. The outnumbered American troops were able to retreat in spite of the British attempt to cut them off.

The next day, the rain stopped the fighting. During the night of August 29–30, the Americans quietly moved their forces from Long Island to Manhattan. This unexpected move took the British completely by surprise. The Americans survived to fight another day. However, the British went on to capture New York City.

Refer to the battle map and answer the following questions.

1. Which of the two armies had the superior force?
   the British

2. Describe the three areas where the American troops were located at the beginning of the battle.
   the Heights of Guan and Brooklyn Heights on Long Island and New York City on Manhattan Island

28

---

3. Name the British commanders involved in the battle.
   Grant, von Heister, Howe, Clinton, Cornwallis, Percy

4. Name the American commanders.
   Alexander, Sullivan, Miles, Putnam, and Washington

5. What were the British troops approaching from the east trying to accomplish?
   They wanted to cut off the Americans from retreat to Brooklyn Heights.

6. How was the British victory incomplete?
   The British failed to cut off the American retreat to Brooklyn Heights.

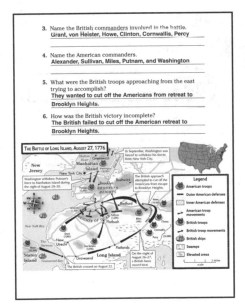

29

LESSON 5 · Learn about Cultural History

Something to Think About

How has history influenced the place where you live?

Americans are united by their cultural history. This includes the common experiences and beliefs that we share. Did you know that many of the beliefs we share today came from the time of the Revolutionary War? Some of them are expressed in the Declaration of Independence written in 1776.

Refer to the excerpts from the Declaration of Independence on Appendix page 101. Answer the following questions.

1. What is the Preamble to the Declaration of Independence?
   The Preamble explains why the 13 states are declaring separation or independence from Britain.

2. What are "inalienable rights"? List some of them.
   Inalienable rights are the natural rights that all people have. They include life, liberty, and the pursuit of happiness.

3. Why are governments created?
   Governments are created to protect the natural rights that all people have.

30

---

4. What is the proper way to form a government?
   Governments should be formed by the consent of the governed (that is, the people).

5. What do the people have the right to do if the government does not protect and respect their rights?
   The people can overturn the government and create a new one.

6. Describe three grievances in the Declaration of Independence.
   Possible answer: Britain has cut off trade between the states and other parts of the world, imposed taxes without the consent of the people, and denied the people trial by jury.

Think about the history of your region of the United States. Do some research to learn about a person or event that is part of your cultural history. Below are ways to get some ideas.

7. Find out if there is a festival in your community or state that celebrates the memory of an important event. If so, find out the story behind this celebration and write it in the space below or on a separate piece of paper.
   Answers will vary.

8. Find landmarks in your town. They may be historic buildings, parks, memorials, battle sites, or historic forts or settlements. What is the story behind the landmarks? Write it in the space below or on a separate piece of paper.
   Answers will vary.

31

Answer Key

Page 34

LESSON 6

Build Your Map Skills

Compare Maps with Different Scales

A **canal** is a human-made waterway. The Illinois & Michigan Canal was completed in 1848. It ran 97 miles between Chicago and Peru, Illinois. The canal allowed water travel from the Great Lakes to the Mississippi River and to ports south all the way to the Gulf of Mexico. A total of 15 **locks** were built on the canal. The locks adjusted water levels for boats to allow them to travel the length of the canal.

In an age before railroads, the canal allowed Chicago to become the transportation center of the nation. Within 10 years after the canal opened, the city's population increased 600 percent. Communities along the canal route also prospered.

Today, much of the canal is a park. The Illinois & Michigan Canal National Heritage Corridor preserves the history of the canal and its regional importance.

Refer to the map and answer the following questions.

1. Refer to Map Part A. Name all the communities along the Illinois & Michigan Canal from east to west.
Chicago, Willow Springs, Lemont, Lockport, Joliet, Channahon, Morris, Seneca, Marseilles, Ottawa, LaSalle, and Peru

2. Describe what Map Part B shows. What communities are shown in Map Part B?
Map Part B shows the eastern portion of the canal from just east of Channahon to Seneca. It shows the communities of Channahon, Morris, and Seneca.

34

Page 35

3. Name three things in Map Part B that are not shown in Map Part A.
Possible answer: Map Part B shows roadways and points of interest such as parks and historic sites.

4. Name three things Map Part A shows that Map Part B does not show.
Possible answer: the entire length of the canal; Lake Michigan; and additional communities

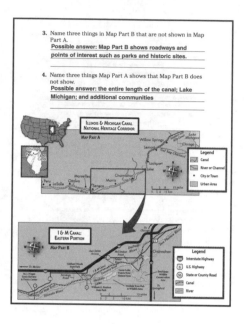

35

Page 37

Select one of the canals mentioned in the passage above. Then, do some library research to complete the table below.

1. Name of canal: **Answers will vary.**
2. Dates of construction: **Answers will vary.**
3. What was the purpose of the canal? What waterways did it link together?
Answers will vary.

4. What products were shipped on the canal?
Answers will vary.

5. Did the canal affect economic growth? How?
Answers will vary.

6. Is the canal still in use? If so, how is it used today?
Answers will vary.

7. After you have completed the table, draw a map of the canal you chose on a separate piece of paper. Use the map of the Illinois & Michigan Canal on page 35 as a guide. Below are some guidelines:
   • If possible, draw the entire length of the canal.
   • Label the communities located along the canal.
   • Identify important waterways that the canal links together.
   • Include a map legend and a compass rose.

37

Page 40

LESSON 7

Build Your Map Skills

Identify Landforms and Water Forms

According to their own history, the Chippewa were the first people to live in the Apostle Islands region. Their main home was Madeline Island, but they used resources from all of the islands. They fished year-round. They also used sugar from the abundant maple trees and gathered plants, such as leeks, fiddleheads, berries, and wintergreen, for both food and medicine. Bark from the white birch tree was used to make wigwams and canoes.

Beginning in the 1800s, the U.S. government began establishing areas called *reservations* for the Chippewa. In 1854, the final treaty between the Chippewa and the U.S. government created the Red Cliff Indian Reservation. Today, almost 1,000 people, mostly Native Americans, live on the reservation.

In 1970, the National Park Service created the Apostle Islands National Lakeshore area. The purpose of the park is to protect the region's wilderness and help the local economy of the Chippewa by promoting tourism.

Refer to the map on the next page and answer the following questions.

1. In what state are the Apostle Islands located? In what lake are the Apostle Islands located?
The islands are in Wisconsin in Lake Superior.

2. Identify at least four water forms shown on the map.
Possible answer: river, lake, bay, channel

40

Page 41

3. Identify at least two landforms shown on the map.
Possible answer: island and peninsula

4. Which bays border the Red Cliff Indian Reservation? What points are included in it?
Raspberry and Frog bays border it. Point Detour, Raspberry Point, and Red Cliff Point are part of reservation.

5. What two towns are located on the Bayfield Peninsula? Which one of these allows access to the islands?
The towns are Red Cliff and Bayfield. Bayfield has ferries or boat rentals that allow access to the islands.

6. Which islands have lighthouses?
Sand Island, Devils Island, Raspberry Island, Michigan Island, and Outer Island have lighthouses.

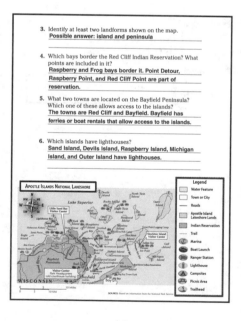

41

Page 42

LESSON 7

Preserve the Natural Areas

Something to Think About

What natural areas near your home are worth preserving?

In this lesson, you have learned about some natural areas that people want to protect. Now, think about the part of the country where you live. Are there any natural areas nearby that you think are worth preserving?

1. Write down at least three natural areas in your community, state, or region that you would like to see maintained for the future. These might be natural features such as rivers, waterfalls, islands, forests, deserts, meadows, or other wild areas. These areas might already be part of a park or other protected zone. Or they might just be some nearby natural areas that you know about and love.
Answers will vary.

2. Do some library research to find out at least two types of plants and two types of animals that live in the natural areas you want to protect. Write the information on the lines below.
Answers will vary.

42

Answer Key

Panel 43:

3. If these areas are not protected, what do you think might happen to them? Use the lines below to describe how they might become endangered over time.
Answers will vary.

4. Ask at least three adults if they know about the areas you want to protect. What do these areas mean to them? Do they agree that the areas should be protected? Why or why not? Write what you find out on the lines below.
Answers will vary.

5. Now that you have collected some information, write a paragraph describing why the natural areas are worth preserving.
Answers will vary.

43

Panel 46:

LESSON 8

Build Your
Map Skills

Understand the Great Flood of 1993

The Mississippi River and its tributaries are considered to be the Mississippi River drainage basin. This basin drains a wide area of the central United States.

When a river or stream becomes so full that it flows over its banks, it is **flooding**. Every year, floods spoil drinking water and destroy homes, businesses, and crops.

Every stream and river floods from time to time, so floods are natural events. One main reason for flooding is heavy or long-lasting precipitation. **Precipitation** is liquid water (rain) or solid water (ice or snow) that falls to Earth.

Dams and **levees** are barriers that people build to hold back or control the flow of water. Sometimes, rainfall is so great that floods overwhelm all the levees and dams. This happened during the Great Flood of 1993.

Use the map and chart to answer the questions.

1. Which states were affected by the flood of 1993?
North Dakota, South Dakota, Nebraska, Kansas, Minnesota, Wisconsin, Iowa, Missouri, and Illinois were all affected by the flood of 1993.

2. What comparison is made in the chart?
The chart compares the normal and the actual amounts of precipitation for the Upper Mississippi River basin during several months of 1992 and 1993.

46

Panel 47:

3. How much rain does the region usually receive in June? How much actually fell in June of 1993?
The region usually receives 4 inches of rain in June. In June 1993, 7 inches actually fell.

4. Approximately how much precipitation actually fell in the region from January to August 1993? Approximately how much falls during these months in a normal year?
About 34 inches actually fell; about 22½ inches usually falls.

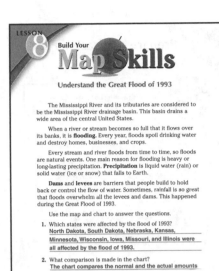

47

Panel 48:

LESSON 8

Learn about Tributaries

Something to **Think** About — How do tributaries create a river system?

The map on page 49 shows the headwaters of the Mississippi River along with some if its major tributaries.

All rivers flow in a certain direction because of changes in **elevation**, or the height of the land. **Headwaters** are where a stream begins.

1. Complete the table. List each tributary on the map in the order in which it enters the Mississippi, from north to south.

Name of Tributary	General Direction that the River Flows	The River Drains What States on the Map?
Minnesota River	southeast, then northeast	Minnesota, South Dakota
St. Croix River	southwest	Wisconsin, Minnesota
Chippewa River	southwest	Wisconsin
Wisconsin River	southwest	Wisconsin
Iowa River	southeast	Iowa
Des Moines River	southeast	Iowa, Minnesota
Illinois River	west, then southwest	Illinois, Indiana
Missouri River	east, southeast, then east	South Dakota, Nebraska, Iowa, Kansas, Missouri
Kaskaskia River	southwest	Illinois
Ohio River	southwest	Indiana, Illinois, Kentucky

48

Panel 49:

2. What lake is at the Mississippi headwaters?
Lake Itasca

Pick one of the tributaries shown on the map and do library research to learn more about it.

3. What is the name of the river you have selected?
Answers will vary.

4. Where does it begin? Where does it end?
Answers will vary.

5. Name some communities located along the tributary.
Answers will vary.

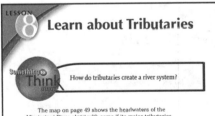

49

Panel 52:

LESSON 9

Build Your
Map Skills

Understand a Natural Disaster

During the months of late summer and fall, hurricanes pose a threat to many people who live along the southeast coast from Texas to North Carolina.

Hurricanes gather heat and energy from the warm waters of the Atlantic Ocean and Gulf of Mexico. The storms move in a counterclockwise direction around an "eye," which is a calm center area 20 to 30 miles wide. The storm may extend as much as 400 miles from the eye.

Hurricanes have winds of at least 74 miles per hour. When they come onto land, the heavy rain, violent winds, and high waves can cause major destruction. Communities where hurricanes are likely to strike must develop plans for dealing with such storms.

In August 2005, a very big hurricane named Katrina hit the southeast coast along the Gulf of Mexico. Florida, Mississippi, Alabama, and Louisiana suffered major destruction. Many communities were flooded. More than 1,400 people were killed and another 1.5 million people had to leave their damaged homes.

Refer to the map and answer the following questions.

1. The map shows parts of which states?
Louisiana and Mississippi

2. Which state did Katrina touch first when it hit land?
Louisiana

52

Answer Key

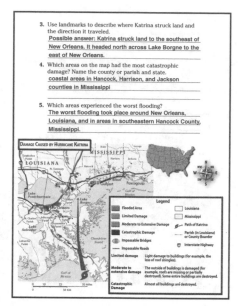

3. Use landmarks to describe where Katrina struck land and the direction it traveled.
   Possible answer: Katrina struck land to the southeast of New Orleans. It headed north across Lake Borgne to the east of New Orleans.

4. Which areas on the map had the most catastrophic damage? Name the county or parish and state.
   coastal areas in Hancock, Harrison, and Jackson counties in Mississippi

5. Which areas experienced the worst flooding?
   The worst flooding took place around New Orleans, Louisiana, and in areas in southeastern Hancock County, Mississippi.

53

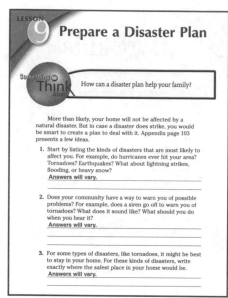

LESSON 9

Prepare a Disaster Plan

Something to Think About — How can a disaster plan help your family?

More than likely, your home will not be affected by a natural disaster. But in case a disaster does strike, you would be smart to create a plan to deal with it. Appendix page 103 presents a few ideas.

1. Start by listing the kinds of disasters that are most likely to affect you. For example, do hurricanes ever hit your area? Tornadoes? Earthquakes? What about lightning strikes, flooding, or heavy snow?
   Answers will vary.

2. Does your community have a way to warn you of possible problems? For example, does a siren go off to warn you of tornadoes? What does it sound like? What should you do when you hear it?
   Answers will vary.

3. For some types of disasters, like tornadoes, it might be best to stay in your home. For these kinds of disasters, write exactly where the safest place in your home would be.
   Answers will vary.

54

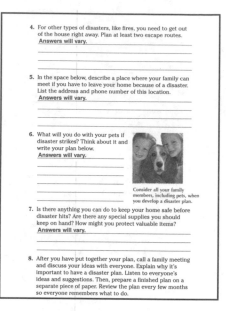

4. For other types of disasters, like fires, you need to get out of the house right away. Plan at least two escape routes.
   Answers will vary.

5. In the space below, describe a place where your family can meet if you have to leave your home because of a disaster. List the address and phone number of this location.
   Answers will vary.

6. What will you do with your pets if disaster strikes? Think about it and write your plan below.
   Answers will vary.

   Consider all your family members, including pets, when you develop a disaster plan.

7. Is there anything you can do to keep your home safe before disaster hits? Are there any special supplies you should keep on hand? How might you protect valuable items?
   Answers will vary.

8. After you have put together your plan, call a family meeting and discuss your ideas with everyone. Explain why it's important to have a disaster plan. Listen to everyone's ideas and suggestions. Then, prepare a finished plan on a separate piece of paper. Review the plan every few months so everyone remembers what to do.

55

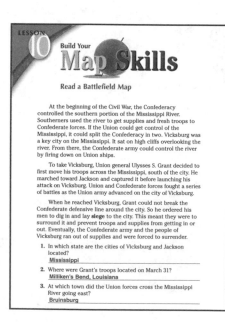

LESSON 10

Build Your Map Skills

Read a Battlefield Map

At the beginning of the Civil War, the Confederacy controlled the southern portion of the Mississippi River. Southerners used the river to get supplies and fresh troops to Confederate forces. If the Union could get control of the Mississippi, it could split the Confederacy in two. Vicksburg was a key city on the Mississippi. It sat on high cliffs overlooking the river. From there, the Confederate army could control the river by firing down on Union ships.

To take Vicksburg, Union general Ulysses S. Grant decided to first move his troops across the Mississippi, south of the city. He marched toward Jackson and captured it before launching his attack on Vicksburg. Union and Confederate forces fought a series of battles as the Union army advanced on the city of Vicksburg.

When he reached Vicksburg, Grant could not break the Confederate defensive line around the city. So he ordered his men to dig in and lay **siege** to the city. This meant they were to surround it and prevent troops and supplies from getting in or out. Eventually, the Confederate army and the people of Vicksburg ran out of supplies and were forced to surrender.

1. In which state are the cities of Vicksburg and Jackson located?
   Mississippi

2. Where were Grant's troops located on March 31?
   Milliken's Bend, Louisiana

3. At which town did the Union forces cross the Mississippi River going east?
   Bruinsburg

58

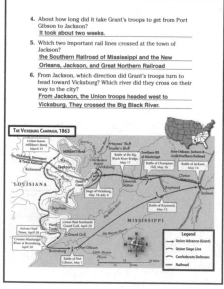

4. About how long did it take Grant's troops to get from Port Gibson to Jackson?
   It took about two weeks.

5. Which two important rail lines crossed at the town of Jackson?
   the Southern Railroad of Mississippi and the New Orleans, Jackson, and Great Northern Railroad

6. From Jackson, which direction did Grant's troops turn to head toward Vicksburg? Which river did they cross on their way to the city?
   From Jackson, the Union troops headed west to Vicksburg. They crossed the Big Black River.

59

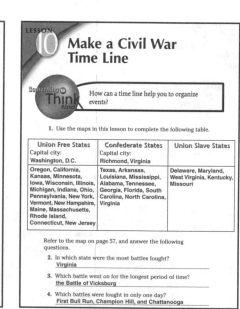

LESSON 10

Make a Civil War Time Line

Something to Think About — How can a time line help you to organize events?

1. Use the maps in this lesson to complete the following table.

Union Free States	Confederate States	Union Slave States
Capital city: **Washington, D.C.**	Capital city: **Richmond, Virginia**	
Oregon, California, Kansas, Minnesota, Iowa, Wisconsin, Illinois, Michigan, Indiana, Ohio, Pennsylvania, New York, Vermont, New Hampshire, Maine, Massachusetts, Rhode Island, Connecticut, New Jersey	Texas, Arkansas, Louisiana, Mississippi, Alabama, Tennessee, Georgia, Florida, South Carolina, North Carolina, Virginia	Delaware, Maryland, West Virginia, Kentucky, Missouri

Refer to the map on page 57, and answer the following questions.

2. In which state were the most battles fought?
   Virginia

3. Which battle went on for the longest period of time?
   the Battle of Vicksburg

4. Which battles were fought in only one day?
   First Bull Run, Champion Hill, and Chattanooga

60

Answer Key

Page 61

5. A **time line** can help to organize key historical events over a period of time. Time lines show events in **chronological order** (in the order the events happened). Use the map on page 57 to make a time line for important Civil War battles. Record the information in the table below.

Name of Battle	Date of Battle (from first to last)	State Where Battle Was Fought
First Bull Run	July 21, 1861	Virginia
Fort Donelson	Feb. 11–16, 1862	Tennessee
Shiloh	April 6–7, 1862	Tennessee
Second Bull Run	Aug. 28–30, 1862	Virginia
Antietam	Sept. 16–18, 1862	Maryland
Fredericksburg	Dec. 11–15, 1862	Virginia
Chancellorsville	April 30–May 6, 1863	Virginia
Champion Hill	May 16, 1863	Mississippi
Vicksburg	May 18–July 4, 1863	Mississippi
Gettysburg	July 1–3, 1863	Pennsylvania
Chattanooga	Aug. 21, 1863	Tennessee
Chickamauga	Sept. 19–20, 1863	Georgia
Wilderness	May 5–7, 1864	Virginia
Spotsylvania	May 8–21, 1864	Virginia

6. Select one of the battles listed in the time line above, and do some library research to learn more about it. Write two or three paragraphs about the battle on a separate piece of paper. Be sure to answer the following questions:
   - When and where did the battle occur?
   - Who were the leading generals?
   - Why was the battle important?
   - How many soldiers lost their lives in the battle?
   - How many soldiers were wounded?
   - Was the battle a clear victory for the Union or for the Confederacy? If neither, explain.

61

Page 65

Refer to the map and answer the following questions.

1. Coronado traveled through which present-day states within the United States?
   Arizona, New Mexico, Texas, Oklahoma, and Kansas

2. Coronado traveled through the lands of what Native American tribes? Name three of them.
   Possible answer: Apache, Navaho, Cheyenne

3. About how far did Cárdenas travel from Háwikuh on his journey to the Grand Canyon?
   about 225 miles

4. Name at least four rivers Coronado's party crossed.
   Possible answer: the San Pedro, Rio Grande, Pecos, and Arkansas rivers

5. According to "the Turk," in which present-day state was Quivira, the "city of gold"?
   Kansas

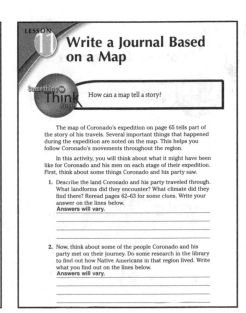

65

Page 66

LESSON 11

Write a Journal Based on a Map

Something to Think about

How can a map tell a story?

The map of Coronado's expedition on page 65 tells part of the story of his travels. Several important things that happened during the expedition are noted on the map. This helps you follow Coronado's movements throughout the region.

In this activity, you will think about what it might have been like for Coronado and his men on each stage of their expedition. First, think about some things Coronado and his party saw.

1. Describe the land Coronado and his party traveled through. What landforms did they encounter? What climate did they find there? Reread pages 62–63 for some clues. Write your answer on the lines below.
   Answers will vary.

2. Now, think about some of the people Coronado and his party met on their journey. Do some research in the library to find out how Native Americans in that region lived. Write what you find out on the lines below.
   Answers will vary.

66

Page 67

3. Assume that you are traveling with Coronado. Use the information you gathered to write a journal about your adventures. Use the map and description of the expedition on pages 64–65 for reference. Below are some points you may want to address in your journal.
   - What was the long journey like through the desert wilderness of Mexico and Arizona to Háwikuh?
   - How did you feel upon finding that Háwikuh was just a pueblo with no gold?
   - What was the reaction of the Cárdenas party upon discovering the Grand Canyon of the Colorado River?
   - Describe the expedition's renewed hope for riches after talking to "the Turk" about Quivira.
   - Describe the long journey from Tiguex across the mountains to the plains of Kansas.
   - What were your thoughts when you found that the Turk had lied about Quivira?
   - How did you feel during your return trip to Mexico, knowing that your expedition had failed?

   Write at least two paragraphs describing the expedition. Use the lines below for your journal entries.
   Answers will vary.

67

Page 70

LESSON 12

Build Your Map Skills

Learn about the Nez Perce Trail

In the early 1800s, the lands of the Native American tribe called the *Nez Perce* spread through Idaho, Oregon, and Washington. In 1855, the tribe even worked with whites to create a reservation in the Wallowa Valley in parts of Oregon, Washington, and Idaho. But when gold was found on Nez Perce land in 1863, the U.S. government took millions of acres from the tribe and tried to force it onto a small reservation in Idaho.

In 1877, General Oliver Howard threatened to attack if the Nez Perce did not move to the Idaho reservation. Chief Joseph and a few hundred Nez Perce followers began traveling toward the reservation. But they soon learned that some Nez Perce warriors had killed several white settlers. A group of soldiers began chasing the Nez Perce as they fled toward freedom in Canada.

Refer to the map and answer the following questions.

1. Where did Chief Joseph's journey begin and end?
   It began in northeastern Oregon near Wallowa Lake. It ended at Bear's Paw Battleground south of Milk River.

2. About how close did Chief Joseph and the Nez Perce get to the Canadian border?
   They got to within about 40 miles of the border.

3. What happened at Camas Meadows Battleground?
   The army lost many horses and mules and was defeated in an attack by the Nez Perce.

70

Page 71

4. What happened at Bear's Paw Battleground?
   Most of the Nez Perce were surrounded, and they surrendered. A small group escaped to Canada.

5. Where did the army finally move Chief Joseph?
   to the Colville Reservation in Washington State

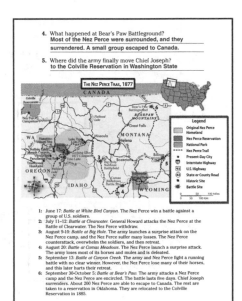

1: June 17: *Battle at White Bird Canyon.* The Nez Perce win a battle against a group of U.S. soldiers.
2: July 11–12: *Battle at Clearwater.* General Howard attacks the Nez Perce at the Battle of Clearwater. The Nez Perce withdraw.
3: August 9–10: *Battle at Big Hole.* The army launches a surprise attack on the Nez Perce camp, and the Nez Perce suffer many losses. The Nez Perce counterattack, overwhelm the soldiers, and then retreat.
4: August 20: *Battle at Camas Meadows.* The Nez Perce launch a surprise attack. The army loses most of its horses and mules and is defeated.
5: September 13: *Battle at Canyon Creek.* The army and Nez Perce fight a running battle with no clear winner. However, the Nez Perce lose many of their horses, and this later hurts their retreat.
6: September 30–October 5: *Battle at Bear's Paw.* The army attacks a Nez Perce camp and the Nez Perce are encircled. The battle lasts five days. Chief Joseph surrenders. About 200 Nez Perce are able to escape to Canada. The rest are taken to a reservation in Oklahoma. They are relocated to the Colville Reservation in 1885.

71

Answer Key

Page 72

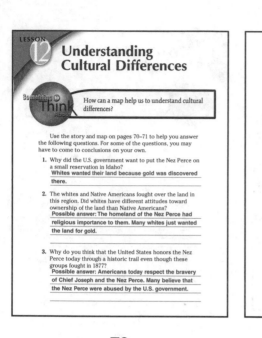

LESSON 12
Understanding Cultural Differences

Something to Think About

How can a map help us to understand cultural differences?

Use the story and map on pages 70–71 to help you answer the following questions. For some of the questions, you may have to come to conclusions on your own.

1. Why did the U.S. government want to put the Nez Perce on a small reservation in Idaho?
   Whites wanted their land because gold was discovered there.

2. The whites and Native Americans fought over the land in this region. Did whites have different attitudes toward ownership of the land than Native Americans?
   Possible answer: The homeland of the Nez Perce had religious importance to them. Many whites just wanted the land for gold.

3. Why do you think that the United States honors the Nez Perce today through a historic trail even though these groups fought in 1877?
   Possible answer: Americans today respect the bravery of Chief Joseph and the Nez Perce. Many believe that the Nez Perce were abused by the U.S. government.

72

Page 73

4. Why do you think Chief Joseph and his followers fled toward Canada after hearing that some Nez Perce had attacked white settlers?
   Possible answer: Chief Joseph's group feared that soldiers would attack them to retaliate.

5. Was Chief Joseph ever able to return to his homeland in the Wallowa Valley?
   No. After he was captured at Bear's Paw, he and most of his followers were sent to Oklahoma. They were later sent to a reservation in Washington state, several hundred miles from the Wallowa Valley.

Now pick a research topic to learn more about Nez Perce history and culture. Choose one of the following topics (or think of one of your own) and do some library research. Write a paragraph about your topic on a separate piece of paper. Some projects may require you to do a sketch or draw a map.

- What did Nez Perce homes look like in the 1800s? How were they built?

- What foods did the Nez Perce eat? Describe how they were cooked and prepared.

- What games did the Nez Perce children play? Describe their favorite toys.

- Find out where most Nez Perce live today. Show some of these locations on a map you create.

- Describe and/or draw traditional Nez Perce clothing.

- Create a time line showing the important events in the life of Chief Joseph.

- Describe the kinds of tools the Nez Perce people used.

- Find out about the Nez Perce tribal flag. Create your own version and explain what it means.

- Learn how the Nez Perce got that name. Find out what they call themselves.

73

Page 76

LESSON 13
Build Your Map Skills

Read a Map to Learn about a Natural Event

The Cascade Range of the northwestern United Sates is volcanic. A **volcano** is a mountain where **magma** (hot, liquefied rock) can erupt through Earth's surface. (Refer to Appendix page 105 to learn more about volcanoes.)

Early on May 18, 1980, Mount St. Helens in Washington State erupted (exploded violently). The power of the blast was enormous. Many square miles of forest were blown down or buried under ashes and rocks. Thousands of animals were killed. Creeks and rivers were clogged with mud. The eruption killed 57 people and destroyed 200 homes.

It's hard to believe, but plant and animal life has returned to the area. By now, more than 25 years later, much of the area is green again.

Use the maps to answer the following questions.

1. Name three communities on the map that may have been in danger during the Mount St. Helens eruption.
   Possible answer: Cougar, Kelso, Kalama

2. Name two lakes located within the Mount St. Helens Monument.
   Coldwater Lake and Spirit Lake

3. Describe the location of monument headquarters.
   It is south of the monument near Amboy.

76

Page 77

4. In one sentence, describe what Map 2 shows.
   Possible answer: It shows the types of destruction caused by the Mount St. Helens eruption.

5. What rivers and creeks were mostly destroyed as a result of the eruption?
   the North and South Fork of Toutle River, Swift Creek, Muddy River, and Smith Creek

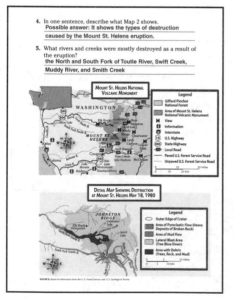

77

Page 78

LESSON 13
Read a Picture Graph

Something to Think About

What can picture graphs tell about natural events?

A **picture graph** can help you to organize and understand events that take place over time. The picture graph on page 79 gives some information about volcanoes. Use the graph to answer the following questions.

1. What does the graph show?
   the major eruptions of volcanoes in the Cascade Mountains over the past 4,000 years

2. In which states are these volcanoes located?
   Washington, Oregon, and California

3. Of all the volcanoes shown on the map, which one has had the most eruptions? How many has it had?
   St. Helens has had the most. It has had 14 eruptions.

4. Which volcano has had the fewest eruptions? Which has had the most recent eruptions?
   Crater Lake and Jefferson have had no eruptions. Shasta, Lassen, and St. Helens have had the most recent.

5. About how long has it been since Newberry has last erupted?
   about 1,000 years

78

Page 79

Learn more about the science and the effects of volcanoes. Refer to the Diagram of a Volcano on Appendix page 105 and the information on pages 76–77. Answer the following question.

6. How do volcanoes cause damage?
   Possible answer: The lava flow can destroy anything it contacts; gases can kill animals and human beings; the power of an explosion can flatten whole forests and homes. Mudflows and ash can foul waterways.

7. Now you will do research in the library to learn more about volcanoes. On a separate piece of paper, write at least two short paragraphs about one of the following volcanic eruptions:
   - Kilauea (1983)
   - Mauna Loa (1984)
   - Lassen Peak (1921)
   - Katmai (1912)

In your report, tell where the volcano is located and when it erupted, the history of the volcano, and the effect on the people who lived near the eruption.

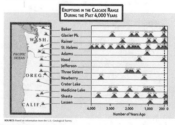

79

Answer Key

[Page 83]

Refer to the map and answer the following questions.

1. Which trail leads to Happy Camp? Name the camps you would pass through on the way from Dyea to Happy Camp.
   Chilkoot Trail leads from Dyea to Happy Camp. Finnigan's Point, Canyon City, Pleasant Camp, and Sheep Camp and the scales are on the way.

2. About how far is it from Dyea to Chilkoot Pass? From Dyea to Bennett?
   Dyea to Chilkoot Pass: 16i miles; Dyea to Lake Bennett: 33 miles.

3. Which trail is the shortest route to Bennett?
   Chilkoot Trail

4. Which trail does the railroad line follow?
   The railroad line follows White Pass Trail.

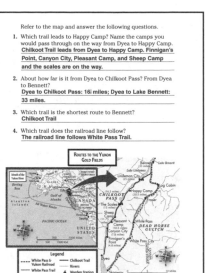

83

[Page 84]

LESSON 14 — Klondike Adventures

Something to Think About: Why did people leave their homes to risk danger in the wilderness?

Answer these questions about the Klondike Gold Rush and the people who traveled to the Yukon. If necessary, do some library research to help answer the questions.

1. What do you think it was like for the prospectors who crossed the mountains from Skagway and Dyea to the gold fields? What hardships did they face?
   Possible answer: It was often very cold and dangerous in the mountain passes. Horses and prospectors were quickly exhausted. Also, some drowned on their way down the Yukon River toward Dawson City.

2. What kinds of people do you think became prospectors? Do you think they were well-prepared for life in the gold fields?
   Possible answer: All kinds of people went to the Klondike, including adventurers and people hoping to provide for their families. Most were not well prepared. Many did not have adequate supplies. Some drowned or died from exhaustion or exposure to the cold.

3. Did most prospectors get rich in the gold fields?
   Possible answer: No. Most prospectors found that the best areas around Dawson City were already claimed. Many just turned around and went home.

84

[Page 85]

4. What tools did miners use to search for gold?
   The basic tools used in the Klondike Gold Rush were rocker boxes, gold pans, blowers, and sluice boxes.

5. Who else besides prospectors might have made money from the Klondike Gold Rush?
   Possible answer: Guides or merchants selling supplies to prospectors in or near the gold fields or in cities like Seattle. Also, those providing transportation by ship.

6. One of the routes shown on the maps on page 83 was known as a "rich person's route" to the Yukon. Which route do you think it was? Why?
   The All-Water Route was the "rich person's route." Travel time on this route was much longer than the other routes, and so it cost more money.

7. Why do you think that the Chilkoot Trail is a popular destination for tourists today? Why is this area such an important part of the cultural history of both Canada and Alaska?
   Answers will vary.

Merchants sold trade goods to prospectors at Sheep Camp on the Chilkoot Trail.

85

[Page 88]

LESSON 15 — Build Your Map Skills

Learn about the Attack on Pearl Harbor

In the 1930s, Japan attacked and conquered parts of China and Southeast Asia and many islands in the Pacific Ocean. During this time, Japan began to fear the power of the U.S. Pacific Fleet.

On December 7, 1941, Japan launched a surprise attack on the United States at Pearl Harbor, Hawaii. Almost immediately, the Japanese damaged or sunk several U.S. ships. Ninety minutes after the attack began, it was over.

The Japanese planes were launched from large ships with flat tops called **aircraft carriers.** The main targets at Pearl Harbor were the U.S. aircraft carriers. Fortunately for the United States, the carriers were away during the attack. The Japanese also failed to destroy oil tanks and ship repair facilities at Pearl Harbor. These later became very important to the U.S. war effort.

The attack sunk or damaged 21 U.S. ships. It also damaged or destroyed 323 U.S. airplanes. About 2,400 American servicemen were killed in the attack, along with many civilians. Most of the damaged U.S. ships were later repaired and used in battle against Japan.

Refer to the map, and answer the following questions.

1. From what general direction did the Japanese planes approach the island of Oahu?
   The Japanese attacked from the north.

88

[Page 89]

2. Which airfields did the Japanese attack on Oahu?
   Wheeler, Ewa, Hickam, Bellows, and Kaneohe

3. Where were most of the battleships in relation to Ford Island?
   They were to the east of Ford Island.

4. Name two ships close to the *Arizona.*
   Possible answer: the *Tennessee* and the *Vestal*

5. What does the map tell you about the way U.S. battleships and cruisers are named?
   Battleships are named for states and cruisers for cities.

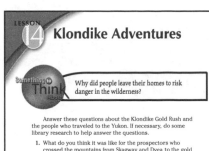

89

[Page 90]

LESSON 15 — World War II and Pearl Harbor

Something to Think About: What can a war memorial tell about history?

Answer these questions about the attack on Pearl Harbor. Refer to Appendix page 106 and the information on the previous pages of this lesson.

1. How was the attack on Pearl Harbor a success for the Japanese? How was it a failure?
   It was successful because it caught the United States by surprise and damaged many ships and planes. It failed because it did not destroy the U.S. aircraft carriers and repair facilities.

2. Why do you think the Japanese wanted to attack the ships within the harbor rather than on the open sea?
   Possible answer: It was easier to locate and attack large numbers of ships anchored close together in the harbor.

3. In the following table, make a list of the U.S. battleships and cruisers at Pearl Harbor during the attack.

Battleships	Cruisers
Pennsylvania, Arizona, Nevada, Oklahoma, Tennessee, California, Maryland, West Virginia	New Orleans, San Francisco, Raleigh, Detroit, Phoenix, Honolulu, St. Louis, Helena

90

Answer Key

4. A **memorial** is something that helps us remember a person or important event. A memorial to the *USS Arizona* sits today in Pearl Harbor. Why do you think special attention is given to the *Arizona?*
   Possible answer: More lives were lost on the *Arizona* than on any other ship at Pearl Harbor. It is important to remember what happened, not only to honor the memory of those who died, but to try to make sure such an attack never happens again.

Do some research to find a war memorial in or near your community. Answer the following questions. If necessary, use a separate piece of paper for your answers.

5. What people or events does the memorial honor? When did these events take place?
   Answers will vary.

6. What does the memorial tell about the people who fought in battle?
   Answers will vary.

This memorial is built over the sunken hull of the *Arizona* at Pearl Harbor.

Photo by PH1(AW) William R. Goodwin

91